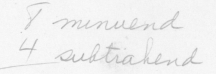

7 minuend
4 subtrahend

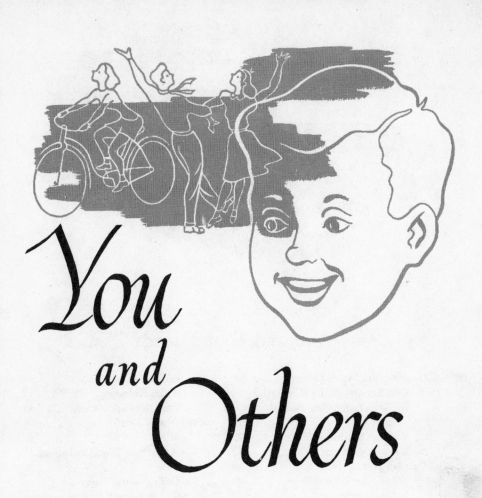

You and Others

by Helen Shacter, Ph.D.
W. W. Bauer, M.D.
Illustrated by Guy Parker, Felix Traugott, and Clara Ernst

HEALTH AND PERSONAL DEVELOPMENT PROGRAM

W. J. Gage and Company Limited
Toronto

Contents

UNIT ONE   You and Your Friends

UNIT TWO You and Your Family

UNIT THREE You and School

3

UNIT FOUR You and Your Community

You and
Your Friends

That Square White Letter

Saturday was always a busy day in downtown Williston, but this Saturday in September was busier than ever. Up and down Main Street, clerks and storekeepers were finishing their decorations for the big week ahead.

The people in Williston were getting ready to celebrate the city's one-hundredth anniversary. A whole week of celebration had been planned. There were to be speeches, a big parade, and parties. The children were preparing special programs, too.

7

Away from Main Street, people were not so busy. But even on quiet streets like Polk Avenue there was some excitement. In every house in this neighborhood where there was a boy or girl from ten to twelve years old, the postman had left a square white letter.

The letter was from Mrs. Arthur Willis, whose family had helped settle Williston years and years ago.

Each letter was an invitation. This is what the letter said.

Dear Neighbor:

I am having a party at my home next Saturday, September 23, at two o'clock. My grandson, Paul, will be here then. So the party is for him and also to help celebrate Williston's one-hundredth anniversary. This will be a Pioneer Party. If you wish, come dressed in a pioneer costume.

Sincerely yours,

Sarah Willis

(Mrs. Arthur Willis)

9

Allen Fuller was sitting on the front porch when the postman handed him his square white letter.

"Well, what do you know!" Allen said aloud, as he read the letter. "Mrs. Willis has a big games room," he thought, "and a party there might be fun if the other fellows are going. I'll see if Bill and Tom got invitations. There ought to be some good things to eat at a party like that!"

Elizabeth Wood looked a little worried after she had read her invitation. "Oh, dear!" she thought. "Mrs. Willis has the nicest house in town, and I'm not sure I know how to *act* at a party there. I don't know what to wear either. Maybe I can borrow one of the pioneer costumes we're using for the program at school, but I—well, I almost wish I hadn't been invited. Still—I'd have felt left out if I hadn't been."

"Oh, who wants to go to an old party anyway!" said Kenneth Williams after he had read his invitation. "I've got better things to do on Saturday than go to a party. But I suppose I'll *have* to go. Mother will make me go when she hears about it."

"Whee!" cried Jane Morrison after reading her invitation. "A party! A party at the Willises! Let's see—maybe I'll wear my blue dress with the white trimming. Or maybe I can think of a pioneer costume to wear. I might—Oh, yes, I *will!* I'll get Grandmother to help me, and I'll go dressed in a way that will surprise everyone. It'll be fun!"

ONE LETTER — MANY FEELINGS!

The postman delivered the same invitation to the homes of eleven other boys and girls in Williston besides Allen, Kenneth, Elizabeth, and Jane. And although it was the same invitation, it was received with many different feelings.

Some boys and girls—like Allen and Jane—were pleased at the thought of going to the party. Others —like Kenneth and Elizabeth—were a little uncertain or unhappy about it.

How would *you* have felt if you had been one of those invited to the party? Would you have felt more nearly like Allen and Jane? Or like Kenneth and Elizabeth?

When Jane discovered how Elizabeth felt about the invitation, she exclaimed, "Why, *everyone* should be glad to go to a party!" Do you agree with Jane?

NO TWO PEOPLE ARE EXACTLY ALIKE

Jane made a mistake that we all make sometimes. She expected others to think and feel the same way that she did. And that isn't always possible. If you stop to think, you can see why. No two of us in all the world are just alike—or have had exactly the same experiences. That's why each one of us may think or feel or act differently from others, even about such little things as invitations to parties. And although it sometimes annoys us when others don't agree with us, we really ought to be glad that they don't. It wouldn't be much fun if everyone talked and acted and felt just alike.

THERE ARE ALWAYS REASONS

When you read about Allen and Jane, you may have thought, "They are the kind who like parties." But did you stop to think *why* they feel as they do about parties? *There are reasons,* you know, for almost everything people say or do or feel.

Allen, for example, had often given parties. He usually had a good time at parties, and he liked to go with his friends to places where there would be fun and "good things to eat." So it was no wonder he was glad to get Mrs. Willis' invitation.

Jane had been to lots of parties, too, and usually she had enjoyed them very much. Her grandmother often made her a new dress for parties. Does this help explain why Jane was happy about the invitation?

Kenneth and Elizabeth had not had such pleasant experiences at parties. So there were some causes for their feelings about the invitation. They both seemed a little unhappy, but they felt that way for different reasons.

The pictures below show some reasons why Kenneth and Elizabeth felt as they did. After looking at the pictures, see if you can explain *why* neither one was very happy about being invited to the party.

Now can you think of some reasons why *you* act and feel as you do when you are invited to a party?

Knowing more about Kenneth and Jane and the others will help you understand them better. In the same way, learning more and more about yourself will help you understand yourself better. It will help you understand that there is usually a reason for the way you feel and act.

Once you can decide what is causing your behavior, you may be able to do something about it. For example, Elizabeth needn't go on worrying about what to do or what to wear at the party. She might talk to some grown person about it—and she might ask her mother to help make over her old party dress. How might Kenneth solve his problem?

As you read *You and Others* you will learn more about the party and other interesting happenings, such as the pioneer program Allen's class gave at school. You will become well acquainted with Kenneth, Allen, Elizabeth, and Jane. You will learn—as they did—different ways of meeting difficulties, of solving problems, and of getting along with others. And you, too, will discover that you *feel* happier when you understand yourself better—and happy feelings are as important to good health as getting plenty of sleep, exercise, fresh air, and good food.

17

"You're Just Mean!"

"Whew!" exclaimed Jane. "I'm all out of breath."

"Say!" puffed Kenneth. "Those early settlers in Williston must have been pretty strong if they could dance the Virginia Reel for a whole evening!"

"How are we doing, Miss Thompson?" asked Elizabeth. "Shall we be ready by Friday night?"

"Oh, yes," Miss Thompson said. "I think your dance will be one of the best parts of the program. I had no idea you boys and girls could learn square dancing so quickly—and so well. Let's rest a moment. Then we'll have time for a little more practice before we go home."

So the boys and girls rested a short while. Then they started to dance once more. But before long it was easy to see that something was wrong. Allen Fuller had stopped dancing, and some of the other boys were dropping out and standing around him.

"Why, Allen!" said Miss Thompson. "Have we tired you out so soon?"

"No-o," Allen answered. "I've decided I don't want to do the dance or be in the program. You can get along without me, all right."

"If Allen won't be in it, I won't," said Bill.

"But the class voted to help with the school program by doing the Virginia Reel," said Miss Thompson. "And it will be much more fun if *everybody* takes part. You think about it tonight, Allen. Maybe you'll feel different tomorrow."

"No, I won't," said Allen. "I know I won't!"

"Well, for goodness' sake! That's a fine thing," cried Jane. "If you aren't in it, I won't have a partner. This is certainly no time to act like that! You'll spoil the whole program. And I think you're just *mean*, Allen Fuller. You're as mean as mean can be!"

WHAT'S THE REASON?

What do *you* think of the way Allen is acting? What reasons has Jane for feeling as she does about Allen's actions?

Now read the conversation that took place between Allen and Miss Thompson the next day. See if it helps you understand better why Allen doesn't want to take part in the program.

Miss Thompson: Well, Allen, have you changed your mind?

Allen: No, Miss Thompson, I don't want to be in the program.

Miss Thompson: But I thought you voted to take part in the program and to learn the Virginia Reel.

Allen: I did, but I wouldn't vote that way now.

Miss Thompson: But there must be some *reason* why you feel as you do.

Allen: Well, there is a reason. I just don't want to dance with a girl!

Miss Thompson: I know how you feel. Lots of boys your age feel that way. Then when they get to high school, they usually change and want to dance with girls every chance they get. But do you think your reason justifies your spoiling the fun for others like Jane, who won't have a partner?

Allen: I wish we hadn't promised to be in it.

Miss Thompson: Sometimes we all have to learn to carry through things that we've promised to do—even if we don't want to. And if you don't take part in the dance you'll cause Bill and maybe others to drop out, too. Soon there might not be enough left for us to have the dance.

Allen: Well, if Bill could be my partner, I wouldn't mind. I really like square dancing.

Miss Thompson: All right, if I can arrange for Bill to be your partner, will you be in the dance?

Allen: Yes, I will.

Miss Thompson: I'll see what I can do.

A GOOD SPORT

"Now," said Miss Thompson, "we must get our costumes ready. Here are some old ones from the storeroom. We'll have to make some of them over."

"What'll *I* wear?" asked Mary, who was Jane's partner now that Bill was dancing with Allen.

"Do you mind dressing as a pioneer boy?" asked Miss Thompson.

"Oh, no," Mary said. "That'll be fun."

"Ho, ho!" laughed Kenneth. "What'll Allen wear?"

"Why, I'll wear the boy's clothes," said Allen, "and Bill can dress as a girl."

"Oh, no, I won't!" cried Bill. "You're the one who made all the fuss, Allen, so *you'll* have to do it!"

"Me?" Allen said. "Oh, no. Not on your life!"

"What a joke!" laughed Jane. "Now don't you wish you had me back as a partner?"

"Come on, Allen," said Don. "Be a good sport and stop making a fuss about things."

"Well-ll," said Allen, "I haven't been a very good sport. But I'd rather dance with a girl than dress like one. So I guess I'll take a girl for a partner."

What was Allen's reason for not wanting to be in the program?

Was it a good enough reason to justify his refusing to coöperate with the others? Why?

What do you think being a good sport means?

What did Allen do that makes you think he was trying to be a good sport after all? What often happens to a person in a group who isn't a good sport?

Hard at Work

"We have only three more days to get these costumes ready for the program," Elizabeth said.

"Is that why the boys are going to sew, too?" asked Peggy. "Because we're in a hurry?"

"No, indeed!" answered Miss Thompson. "Why, some of the boys sew very well and enjoy it! And all of them want to help."

"Goodness!" said Helen. "You should have been in our room last year, Peggy. We did weaving, and the boys made some of the prettiest rugs of all."

"Isn't this yellow dress nice!" exclaimed Elizabeth. "I'm going to borrow it for my pioneer costume to wear to Mrs. Willis' party."

"My party costume is going to be a surprise," Jane said. "But I'd like to have that red dress to make over for our program. I'll ask Miss Thompson for it." And so she did.

But Miss Thompson had already promised to give the red dress to Helen.

So Jane went to the costume box and picked out a brown dress. But she wasn't very happy about it. As she began to sew, she kept thinking, "I don't see why I couldn't have had the red dress. Miss Thompson never gives *me* anything I want!" The more she thought about it, the angrier she felt.

"Jane," said Elizabeth, "may I use your scissors?"

"No, you may not!" snapped Jane. "Can't you see that I need them myself?"

"Well, don't be so cross about it," Elizabeth said. "I'll borrow Helen's."

A little later Jane cried, "Oh-h-h! See what I did! I cut too much off the bottom of my dress. Now it's too short."

"Let's see," said Helen. "Maybe we can help you."

"Nobody can help me," exclaimed Jane. "I'm just stupid, that's all. And my costume is all spoiled."

"You're not stupid," said Elizabeth. "You may not be able to sew as well as some of us, but you do other things lots better. I still get mixed up in the Virginia Reel, but you learned all the steps the very first day. Anyway, I don't think your costume is spoiled. There must be some way to fix it."

The girls looked thoughtfully at the brown dress.

"We could sew back the piece you cut off," said Elizabeth. "But no! I have a better plan. Why not sew on a piece of my yellow goods? The yellow will look pretty on the brown."

"That's a good idea," Jane agreed. "People will think it's supposed to be that way!"

So the three girls got busy, and soon the yellow piece was sewed on.

"Thanks so much," Jane said. "The dress looks fine now. And I'm sorry I was so mean about the scissors, Elizabeth. I really wasn't cross at you. I just don't know why I acted like that!"

Have you, like Jane, ever said something mean or cross to someone who hadn't done a thing to you? Of course you have! And afterward you probably wondered, "Now why did I act like that?"

If you can find reasons for your feelings or your behavior, you can decide whether the way you are acting will help change things you don't like. Sometimes you have very good reasons for acting the way you do. At other times you may need to think of more helpful ways to behave!

There were reasons, for example, why Jane acted as she did about the scissors. But in this case the reasons did not justify her actions toward Elizabeth! Jane was angry at Miss Thompson because she didn't give her the red dress. And without realizing what she was doing, she "took out" her anger on Elizabeth. Then, too, Jane knew she didn't sew very well, and that's probably another reason why she felt out of sorts and ready to take out her anger on the first person who spoke to her.

If Jane had tried, she could have found reasons for the way she acted about the scissors. And then she would have seen that it doesn't help in such situations to snap at people who aren't to blame at all!

Jane might also have comforted herself about her sewing by thinking, "I *do* get a little better each time I sew. Anyway, even if I can't sew as well as the others, I can play the piano pretty well. And I learned square dancing easily."

Of course, you can't help feeling upset and cross at times. When you have such feelings, it's better to talk over what is bothering you than to keep your feelings "bottled up" inside you, as Jane did at first. Talking about them often helps get rid of your upset feelings—and keeps these feelings from coming out in unexpected ways, as Jane's did.

If Jane had told the other girls how disappointed she was about the red dress, they would have understood why she was upset. Just talking about it would have helped Jane get rid of the disappointment, and might have prevented her being cross with Elizabeth about the scissors.

However, "letting off steam" by fussing and grumbling makes you feel better only for a little while. And that's why you will want to learn more worth-while ways of changing upset or angry feelings to more pleasant ones.

When you read the next page you will see why Tom, for example, needed to learn some ways of changing unpleasant feelings to pleasant ones.

No, Tom, you can't go to the movie at the Grand. If you can find a good picture at one of the other theatres, you may go. But the one at the Grand isn't recommended in our movie guide.

Well, if I can't go to the Grand, I'll just sit at home all afternoon.

Look at the pictures above. Why do you think Tom acted as he did? Will his angry actions change the situation he doesn't like?

In the pictures below are shown more helpful ways Tom might have behaved. What are they?

When there is a situation you can't change, instead of feeling angry inside or fussing about it, you will feel better if you forget about it and turn to other things. Get busy doing something you like to do. Find someone else to work or play with. Do something kind for someone.

What situation can you remember when *you* felt "angry inside" and "took out" your mean feelings on someone else? What might you have done instead?

I'll see if I can find a good movie at any of the other theatres.

Come on, Joe. Since I can't see the movie at the Grand, I'll play with you for awhile.

Will you, Tom? That'll be fun! You're such a good player!

FAMILY GUIDE

"You Stole the Show!"

"Look at Jane!" laughed Allen. "She's blushing!"

"I know it!" said Jane. "I always blush when I get excited. I try not to, but I just can't help it!"

"I wish our part of the program would start," said Kenneth. "I hate this waiting around! My hands always get kind of sweaty, and I get a funny feeling in my stomach just before a program starts."

"You ought to feel my heart!" exclaimed Elizabeth. "It's beating fast the way it always does when I get excited. Oh, dear! I know I'll get all mixed up in the dance. I just hope I don't trip or fall or anything. Wouldn't that be *terrible!*"

"I'd stop worrying," advised Allen. "Anyway, in a square dance it's hard for anybody to tell if you *do* get mixed up!"

But Elizabeth didn't take Allen's advice. Even when the dancing on the stage had begun, she kept thinking, "Oh, dear! I know I'll get all mixed up. I know I shall!"

And suddenly, when it was time for her to twirl around with Kenneth, she tripped. But she didn't fall because Kenneth caught her and swung her around.

That pleased the people in the audience, and they began to laugh and to clap.

"Why, people think we're good!" Elizabeth thought in surprise. And after that she stopped worrying. And she didn't trip again either!

"Hi, Strong Man!" Allen said to Kenneth after the program. "Where'd you get that strength?"

"I don't know," laughed Kenneth. "I was so surprised I really didn't know what I was doing!"

"Was it all right?" Elizabeth asked Miss Thompson. "Ken swung me to keep me from falling!"

"All right?" exclaimed Miss Thompson. "Why Elizabeth, you and Kenneth stole the show!"

31

YOUR BODY AND HOW IT WORKS

How did Kenneth and Jane and Elizabeth feel just before taking part in the program?

How do *you* feel before taking part in a program or some other important event?

Perhaps you have noticed at such times that your heart beats faster than it usually does or that blood rushes to your face and neck to make you blush. You may have found that you perspire more freely or that your stomach "feels funny" or that you begin to breathe faster.

Body changes like these that take place when you are excited or worried or angry are quite normal. For the way your body works depends not only on the way you are built but upon the way you *feel*. For example, consider the work of your heart.

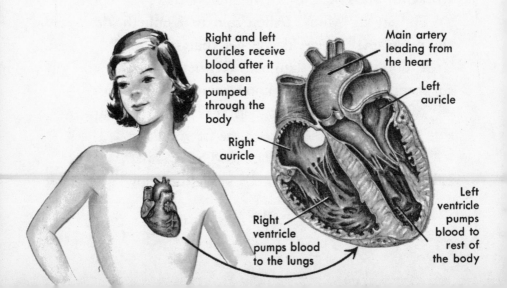

Right and left auricles receive blood after it has been pumped through the body

Main artery leading from the heart

Left auricle

Right auricle

Right ventricle pumps blood to the lungs

Left ventricle pumps blood to rest of the body

YOUR HEART

Each time your heart beats, it forces blood into your arteries, which carry the blood to all parts of the body. The blood flows from the ends of the arteries into the veins through tiny tubes called *capillaries*. The veins carry the blood back to the heart. The picture at the right shows the path the blood takes. The arteries are shown in red and the veins in blue. The blood flowing through the body carries oxygen and digested food to help the parts of the body do their work.

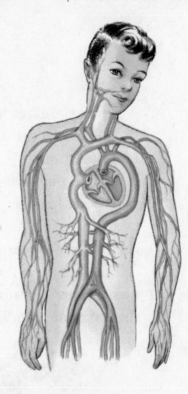

Most of the time your heart beats about 90 times a minute. But the heartbeat may vary with different individuals and in different situations. Exercise makes the heart beat faster. This usually does not harm the heart. But to keep from overworking it, you should rest between periods of hard work and play. When you are excited or upset, your heart often beats faster than usual, too. So you see that your feelings can also affect the way your heart works.

YOUR LUNGS

When you have been exercising hard and begin to breathe faster, you are reminded of the work your lungs are doing.

As you may know, your lungs keep the blood in your body fresh and well supplied with oxygen. You take this oxygen into the lungs with the air you breathe, as shown in the picture at the left below.

The picture at the right below shows the path your blood takes in getting a fresh supply of oxygen from the lungs and sending it out to all parts of the body.

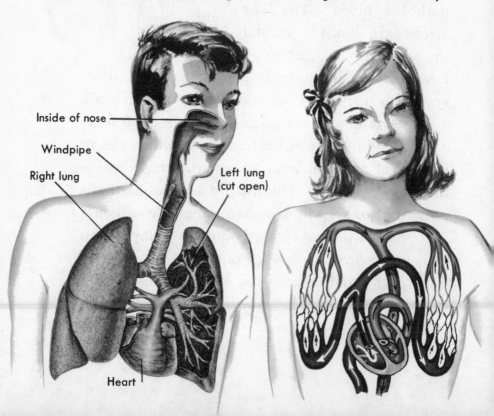

Inside of nose

Windpipe

Right lung

Left lung
(cut open)

Heart

Your lungs work harder than usual when you get excited. When you watch a thrilling game or a dangerous movie scene, you often breathe very fast. This is just another example of how your feelings can affect the way different parts of your body work.

YOUR SKIN

You know that exercise makes the skin perspire more than usual, but did you know that your feelings can make you perspire more freely, too? The little openings, or *pores*, all over your skin are the faucets of your sweat glands. They let out some of the water your body hasn't used. This moisture is called *perspiration*. You perspire all over your body all the time, but most freely in such places as the armpits and the palms of your hands. You may lose from three to five glasses of water a day through perspiration. And at times you may lose even more—times when you are exercising hard, or when you are worried or unsure of yourself.

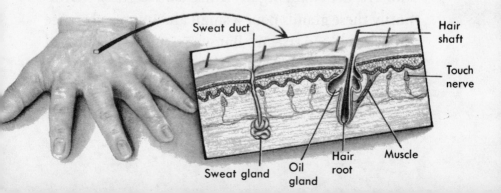

Sweat duct

Hair shaft

Touch nerve

Sweat gland

Oil gland

Hair root

Muscle

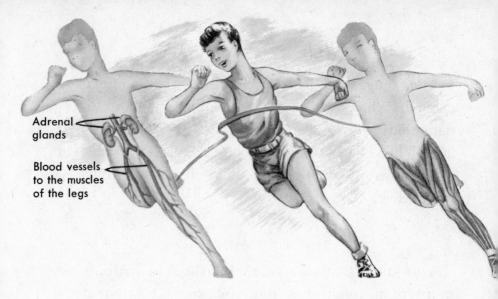

Adrenal glands

Blood vessels to the muscles of the legs

YOUR ADRENAL GLANDS

Have you ever been in a situation where, as Kenneth did in the program, you suddenly found strength that surprised you? Perhaps you have been about to drop out of a race when your friends urged, "Come on! Run! You can win!" And in the excitement you suddenly found you had enough strength to keep you in the race.

In situations like this, it is your emotions that give your muscles more speed and power than usual.

What happens is this. In your body, just above your kidneys, are small organs called *adrenal glands*. Ordinarily these glands pour a small amount of substance into your blood stream. But when you get frightened or angry or excited, they pour out extra substance that quickly gives your muscles greater strength.

YOUR STOMACH AND KIDNEYS

The food you eat is taken care of, or *digested*, by the stomach and other organs shown below. Ordinarily these organs work without trouble or delay.

MOUTH: the saliva here begins to digest food

ESOPHAGUS: this tube takes the food from the mouth to the stomach

STOMACH: the food is mixed with digestive juice and churned here

PANCREAS: digestive juice flows from here into the small intestine

SMALL INTESTINE: here much food is dissolved and passed through the walls of the intestines into the blood stream

RECTUM: the opening from which waste material left over from the food is passed out of the body

LIVER: some food is stored here and digestive juice from here flows into the small intestine

GALL BLADDER: digestive juice also flows from here into the small intestine

LARGE INTESTINE: waste material left over from the food is carried through the large intestines to an opening and passed out of the body

Suppose you eat dinner at six o'clock. Your digestive system will work something like this:

6 P.M.—Your stomach starts its work of mixing and churning the food.

9 P.M.—The food is going into your small intestine.

11 P.M.—Your small intestine is filled, and the food is being dissolved by digestive juices from the liver, gall bladder, and pancreas. The dissolved food is passing through the walls of your small intestine and into your blood stream. Your blood will then carry it to all parts of your body to help you grow, to make repairs that your body needs, and to give you energy. The waste left over from the food is passing into the large intestine.

5 A.M.—The waste materials are part way through your large intestine.

6 A.M. to 12 M.—The waste materials are ready to be passed out of your body by a bowel movement.

Of course you should remember that the time required for digesting food is not the same in all individuals nor the same in any one individual all the time.

If you are well and happy—and if you haven't exercised hard right after eating—these processes all happen without your thinking about them.

But suppose you have been worrying for several days about not doing well at school. Or suppose you are angry and upset because a group of your friends haven't been including you in their plans lately. Then your six o'clock meal—and your other meals—may not be digested in the usual way.

Your upset feelings may interfere with the work of your stomach. Then you may complain of "gas" or heartburn or a stomach ache.

Or you may find that during these periods of worry, excitement, or other upset feelings you have more bowel movements than are usual for you. Or just the opposite may be true; you may have fewer bowel movements and become *constipated*.

You may have noticed, too, that in times of excitement your kidneys do not work as usual. You may urinate more often. And it occasionally happens that boys and girls your age wet the bed at night when they are worried or upset. This bed-wetting is called *enuresis*. You should not worry or feel guilty about enuresis. But you should try to face and solve your problem. Often, talking things over with some grown-up person you like and respect will help you get things straightened out.

Again you see why it is important to know how to change unpleasant feelings to more pleasant ones.

You remember Jane said, "I always blush when I get excited. I try not to, but I just can't help it!"

And Jane was right. Neither she nor you can stop blushing, even if you try. You cannot command the blood to stay out of your head any more than you can order your heart to stop beating.

That is because one part of your nervous system works without your being able to control it at all. This part is called the *autonomic nervous system*. The nerves in the autonomic nervous system take care of the actions of your body that must go on twenty-four hours a day, whether you are awake or asleep. They see that your heart, liver, lungs, stomach, intestines, kidneys, bladder, blood vessels, and your various glands do their work.

You can see why the autonomic nervous system is important. It controls organs of your body that cannot wait for you to think about them before they do their work. These organs have had to work from the very moment you were born, because you had no time to "learn" to breathe or to make your heart beat. That's why one part of your nervous system does nothing but take care of the work of important organs in your body without your having to think about them.

The other part of your nervous system is your *central nervous system*. It is made up of one set of nerves that takes messages from all parts of your body to your brain—and another set of nerves that carries orders from your brain to all parts of your body.

For example, suppose your doorbell rings. One set of nerves carries the sound sensation through your ears to your brain. Your brain interprets the sound as a doorbell ringing and sends orders through the other set of nerves to the muscles of your arms and legs. The orders tell you to walk to the door and open it. The brain also sends orders to your speech organs and then you say, "Hello." Of course, all this happens very fast.

The important difference between your central nervous system and your autonomic nervous system is that you can control one and not the other. For example, you can decide, "I'll stop writing now." And your brain will send orders to the muscles of your fingers to put down the pencil. But you can't decide, "I'll stop my heart beating now," for your autonomic nervous system controls these actions of your organs without your having anything to say about it.

Now turn to pages 42 and 43. The pictures on these pages will give you an even better idea of how the two parts of your nervous system work.

41

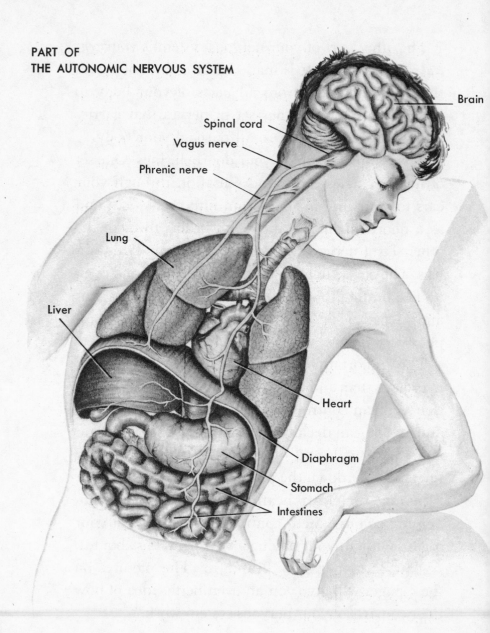

PART OF
THE AUTONOMIC NERVOUS SYSTEM

Brain

Spinal cord

Vagus nerve

Phrenic nerve

Lung

Liver

Heart

Diaphragm

Stomach

Intestines

42

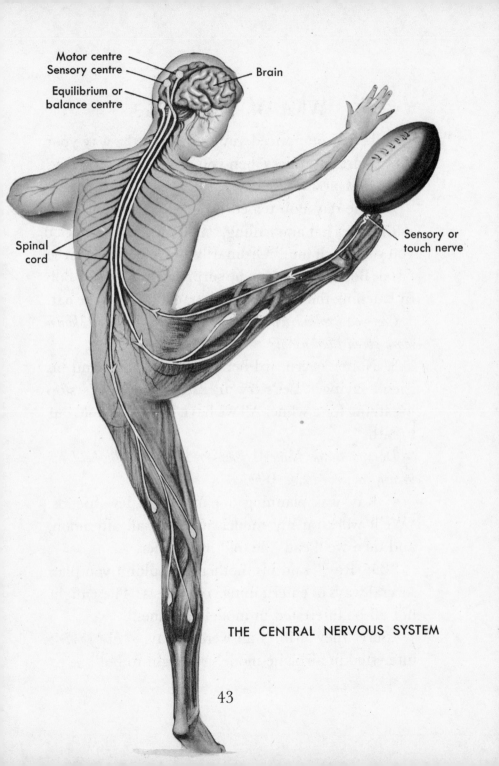

Motor centre
Sensory centre
Equilibrium or
balance centre
Brain

Spinal
cord

Sensory or
touch nerve

THE CENTRAL NERVOUS SYSTEM

43

What Do You Think?

1. Have you noticed any changes in the way your body works at times when you are excited or angry? *What changes take place? How do you explain them?*

2. One day Bob teased little Billy by running off with Billy's hat and calling, "You may have it back if you can catch me!" Ordinarily Billy couldn't run so fast as Bob. But this day he surprised himself *and* Bob by catching the older boy and snatching back the hat.

Can you explain why Billy might suddenly have shown more speed than usual?

3. Nancy overheard her younger brother and his friend saying, "Let's try an experiment. Let's stop breathing for a while. All we have to do is to hold our breath."

Do you think Nancy's younger brother could hold his breath for very long? Why?

4. Ray was planning a party for a few friends. "We'll work on my model airplanes all afternoon, and then we'll eat," he told his mother.

"But, Ray," said his mother, "shouldn't you plan several ways of entertaining your guests? They might not all be interested in model airplanes."

"Sure they will," answered Ray. "*Everybody's* interested in airplane models or ought to be!"

44

Do you agree with Ray? Why? What suggestions would you give him about entertaining his guests?

5. "Come back and put your rubbers on!" called Mary's mother. And Mary did so, but she wasn't very happy about it. Then, as she started down the street, she met her friend Sally.

"Are you going to eat lunch at school?" asked Sally.

"What do you care?" snapped Mary. "If you'd look, you'd see I haven't a lunch box!"

Why do you think Mary snapped at Sally as she did?

What might Mary learn to do to keep from "taking out" her feelings on others who aren't to blame?

6. Jean Fisher had just moved to Williston, and she didn't know anyone in this new town. On her first day at school Betty said to Jean, "Hello, I'm Betty Hill. Did you just move here?"

"Um-hum," answered Jean.

"Do you think you'll like it here?" asked Betty.

"Um-hum," answered Jean.

Later Betty told some of her friends, "That new girl's funny. All she ever says is 'Um-hum.' I don't think we'll want to have much to do with her."

Was Betty fair to the new girl? What makes you think as you do? What might have been some reasons why Jean didn't say much at first? What might Betty have done to make her feel more at ease?

45

Wait and See

"Elizabeth, wait for me!" called Nancy. "I'm going to the Guide meeting, too. I called you once before, but you didn't hear me."

"No, I didn't hear you. I must have been thinking about something," Elizabeth said.

"What were you thinking about?" asked Nancy.

"Well-ll," Elizabeth answered, "I was thinking about Mrs. Willis' party tomorrow—and wishing I knew just how to *act*. I've never gone to a big party like that before."

"Cheer up!" said Nancy. "Before this afternoon is over, you'll know everything you need to know."

"You're just trying to make me feel better," Elizabeth said. "Either that or you're fooling me."

"No, I'm not," laughed Nancy. "I'm telling you the truth. You just wait and see!"

So Elizabeth waited until after the Girl Guide meeting had started. Then she *did* see that Nancy was right.

"We have a surprise program today," Mrs. Winters, the Girl Guide leader, said. "The girls in Nancy's company have been working on the Hostess Merit Badge, and this afternoon they're going to dramatize some of the things they've been learning."

"That's right," said Nancy. "Since some of us are going to a party tomorrow, we thought this would be a good time to dramatize and talk about ways of being a pleasant guest. Some other time we'll talk about ways of being a good hostess."

Then the girls gave their dramatization and their explanations. After they had finished, Elizabeth gave a big sigh of relief.

"Now I *do* know everything I'll need to know," she thought. "And I've learned some things I'd never even thought of before."

Perhaps you, like Elizabeth, have sometimes wondered about what to do or say when you go to a party or go visiting. Most people have. What are some things you have not always been very sure about?

Actually there are only a few things you need to know to make you feel comfortable and at ease. You can learn these things by studying the pictures on pages 49 and 50. These pictures show some of the dramatizations Nancy and her friends gave.

After looking at the pictures carefully, see if you can answer these questions:

1. What are some pleasant greetings to use when you arrive at a friend's home or at a party?

2. How will you usually know where to put your coat and hat? What might you do if you aren't sure?

3. When should two people be introduced?

4. How do introductions help?

5. When you are introduced to someone, what do you say? What might you do to help the person know you are glad to meet him?

6. How would you introduce a boy named Jack Wood to a girl named Helen Brown?

7. What are some courteous ways to say "good-bye" at the end of a party or a visit?

You always feel more comfortable when you know what to do or say. A good way to greet a host or hostess is to say "Hello" and add the person's name. If you are greeting a mother or some other grown-up, it is courteous to say "How do you do?" and then add the person's name.

You don't have to worry about what to do with your wraps. Your host or hostess will tell you where to put them. If for some reason you aren't told, ask politely what you should do with them.

49

Often at a party your host or hostess will introduce you to a stranger. When this happens, all you have to do is to smile pleasantly and say, "How do you do?" If you wish, add the name of the person to whom you are being introduced.

If you are doing the introducing, be sure to say the names of the two persons very plainly. If you are introducing a boy to a girl, it is courteous to say the girl's name first.

When you leave a party—or when you leave a friend's home after visiting there for some time—always say "Good-bye" to the person who invited you. It's also courteous to say "Good-bye" to a mother or some other grown-up who has helped you have a good time. It's pleasant to add something like, "I had a very good time," or "Thank you very much."

THINK LESS ABOUT YOURSELF
AND MORE ABOUT OTHERS!

Have you ever felt the way Kenneth did—that parties aren't much fun because you find you are off by yourself most of the time?

If so, did you ever stop to think that the trouble might be with yourself and not with the party?

Perhaps you have been so busy feeling uncomfortable or sorry for yourself that you haven't taken time to be friendly or to enter into the general fun. With just a little effort you can change this and make party-going lots more fun for yourself.

Nancy and her friends dramatized some things you can do to help you have a good time at parties. The pictures below show some of the dramatizations that they gave.

This isn't any fun—just standing around with nobody to talk to. I don't think people at this party are very friendly.

My, but that's a pretty dress you have on! What game do you think we are going to play next?

DON'T think about yourself all the time. It doesn't help to feel sorry for yourself because you haven't anyone to talk to.

DO find someone to talk to. Making someone else feel at ease will help you, too.

DON'T make things difficult for your host or hostess. Don't be unpleasant about entertainment that is suggested. Others may enjoy it, even if you don't.

DO help your host or hostess by showing interest and willingness to take part. Remember that even if you aren't especially interested in a game, others may be.

DON'T stay away from parties because you think you may not have a good time. It's never helpful to "run away" from your problems.

DO try to make party-going more fun. Go every time you are invited. Be friendly and ready to enjoy yourself. Each time you go, you'll get more confident—and have more fun!

Elizabeth said the dramatizations that Nancy and the others gave, taught her some things she'd never even thought of before. Did you learn some things you didn't know? If so, what were they?

Which suggestions on pages 51 or 52 might be helpful to you? What other advice can you add?

Getting Ready

"Allen," said his mother, "you'd better go back and wash behind your ears. And use the little hand brush to get the dirt off your hands. You just aren't clean enough to go to a party!"

"You're always nagging at me because I'm not clean enough," said Allen.

"Yes, that's true," agreed his mother. "Maybe we ought to make a bargain, Allen. I'll try to stop reminding you so often about being clean if you'll try to remind *yourself* more often."

"I'll try," Allen said, "but I don't see why it matters if I'm not so clean."

"When you're going out to play, it doesn't matter much," said his mother. "But when you're going to school or to church or to a party, it *does* matter. People expect you to be clean and neat then, and they don't think so well of you if you aren't."

"Well, I'll go and wash some more," Allen said. "But I'll bet the other fellows aren't having all this trouble getting ready for a party."

Allen thought he was the only one who was having trouble getting ready for Mrs. Willis' party. But let's see what was happening at his friends' homes.

At Kenneth's house things had got off to a bad start that Saturday morning. Kenneth, you know, hadn't really wanted to go to the party. And when he woke up the day of the party, he had a headache.

"Oh-h! my head hurts!" he said at breakfast. "I don't think I'm going to feel well enough to go to the party this afternoon."

"That's too bad," his mother said. "Maybe you should go back to bed for a while, Kenneth."

"You take it easy today, Ken," said his father. "After lunch your mother and I are driving over to Lake City to do some shopping and maybe see a movie. But we'll be back before dinner. You stay quiet while we're gone."

So Kenneth went back to bed for a while.

At lunch time he said, "I feel better now. Will you take me to Lake City with you, Dad?"

"Next Saturday we will," answered his father. "But if you feel better today, you should go to the party. I know you aren't looking forward to it very much, but staying away won't help you learn to enjoy parties. Anyway, you may have a good time."

"Well, maybe so," said Kenneth. "I'll go and see."

At the Woods' house, Elizabeth's family were "taking a look" at her to see if she was ready for the party.

"Well," Elizabeth said slowly, "I don't look so very glamorous, do I? Do you suppose some of Mother's lipstick would help?"

"No, I don't," said her big brother, Ned. "Anyway, you are dressed as a pioneer woman, and nobody ever thought of wearing lipstick in pioneer days."

"Your shoes are dirty," said Jo Ann.

"Jo Ann's right," said Ned. "And if you want to know what I honestly think, I'll tell you. You can't be glamorous with unshined shoes and dirty fingernails and hair flying all around. Why don't you fix up a bit more and see how much better you'll look?"

So Elizabeth combed and brushed her hair, cleaned her fingernails, and shined her shoes. Then she *did* look better.

All the week before the party, Jane had been arguing with her mother.

"I want to get my hair done at the beauty shop," she kept saying. "*Why* can't I, Mother?"

At last her mother said, "I've told you, Jane, that it's too expensive, especially since there isn't a thing the beauty shop can do that you can't do yourself. Your hair is easy to do, you know. But if you really want to go, I'll let you. Only you'll have to use your own allowance to pay for it."

"Oh, dear!" thought Jane. "I could never save enough out of my allowance for that!"

So on the morning of the party she said, "Mother, will you show me how to pin up my hair the way they do at the beauty shop downtown?"

"Of course," her mother said. "After you wash it!"

Jane shampooed her hair, and her mother helped pin it up. When it was time for the party, Jane looked as pretty as if her hair *had* been done at a beauty shop!

An interesting thing had happened to Kenneth on the day of the party. He didn't want to go to the party, and that morning he woke up with a headache. The first thing he thought was, "I just can't go to the party today. I'm too sick."

Do you think there might have been any connection between Kenneth's headache and his not wanting to go to the party?

Did anything like that ever happen to you?

Maybe you have at one time or another forgotten to do some homework for the next day at school. The following morning you may have found that you felt dizzy and weren't able to go to school. Or maybe you can remember being asked to do a lot of errands for your mother and finding, before the errands were finished, that your knee hurt. This may have kept you from doing all the errands.

What other examples of this kind can you think of?

Things like this happen to you and to everyone at times. You get upset about doing something and before long you may have found a way to avoid doing it! The important thing is to try to see that you don't get into the *habit* of using illness as an excuse to get out of doing things that you don't like to do.

That's why it's a good idea to stop now and then and consider what is making you feel as you do.

George, for example, wasn't very good in spelling, and he hated Friday mornings because of the weekly spelling test. Before long he began to have a stomach ache, and to stay home those mornings. But by noon he usually felt all right again.

Now, of course, George might have had something wrong with his digestion. But if he had, he would have felt ill on other mornings besides Fridays. And his family probably would have taken him to see a doctor. But since his stomach aches always came at the same time, George might well have begun to think, "Am I using a stomach ache to avoid something I don't like?" or "What is it I am trying to avoid on Friday mornings?" Once he discovers and faces the reason for his actions, he can do something to help himself. When he faces the fact that he is trying to avoid the spelling tests, he can then decide to ask for help with his spelling. He can also try to stop thinking, "I hate spelling" and think instead, "I'm going to work harder at my spelling. I know I can do better if I try!"

Another example is the case of Mary. She felt sorry for herself one day when her sister Alice got a new dress, and at dinner she didn't eat much.

She said she wasn't hungry. But if she had faced the truth she would have thought, "I'm unhappy because Alice has a new dress and I haven't." Then she might have changed these unhappy feelings by remembering, "But I *did* get a new hat when Alice didn't."

In the pictures below Harry has become upset and has angrily rushed from the room. Notice that Harry awkwardly knocked over a lamp as he left. Later he said, "That old lamp got in my way!" But there was another reason why Harry had been clumsy. What was it?

What might Harry do to help avoid situations like this?

It's always a good plan to try to recognize what's back of your headache, dizziness, "funny feeling inside," or unusual clumsiness. Then correct the cause if you can. Get help from some older person if necessary. If the situation can't be changed, accept it, try to forget about it, make the best of it!

HOW YOU LOOK

When Allen was getting ready for the party, you remember he had a little trouble. What caused his trouble?

Have you ever had trouble like that or felt that people were "always nagging at you" about being clean and neat? If so, what suggestions did Allen's mother make that might help you put an end to some of this nagging?

What are some of the times when it isn't necessary to be spotlessly neat and clean? What are some of the times when people expect you to be as clean and neat as possible?

Which boys and girls in the picture below look as if they were ready to go to school or a party? What makes you think so?

Are *you* usually clean and neat when you go to school or to church or to a party? If not, how might you help yourself improve?

Allen wasn't the only one who had trouble and delay in getting ready for the party. Elizabeth had been having some troubles, too. What were they?

Which of the articles shown above would have helped Elizabeth get ready? How is each of these articles used? Which ones do *you* often use?

Look at the hands shown below. Which ones show that good use has been made of some of the articles above? Which articles have probably been used on the clean hands? What care do the other hands need?

Which pairs of shoes shown below would be best to wear to school or to church or to a party?

Which shoes need the use of some articles shown above? Which ones need repairing?

Why had Jane been nagging at her mother all the week before the party? How did she and her mother solve Jane's difficulty?

Now look at the pictures above. They show how Jane's mother helped her shampoo her hair. What is happening in each picture? This is the way hair is shampooed in beauty shops, too.

Boys usually wash their hair in just about the same way, only they often wash their hair while taking a bath or a shower.

To keep your hair clean and shining, you should plan to wash it once a week and to brush it well every day.

If you are a girl—and if, like Jane, you don't want to spend your allowance paying the beauty shop to do your hair—the pictures above may help you. They show an easy way to pin up your hair so that it will curl the way you want it when it is dry.

Another thing to remember about your hair is that it can be done in different ways and that some ways may be more becoming to you than others. For example, if you have a very round face, you may find that parting your hair in the centre is not the most becoming style for you.

Notice the different hair styles the girl in the pictures below might use. Which ones do you think are most becoming?

The Party at Last

"Just what I thought," grumbled Kenneth to himself. "This party's no fun—just standing around."

Elizabeth had been thinking the same thing until she suddenly realized how ill at ease Kenneth was. Then she remembered, "If you help someone enjoy himself, you often help yourself, too."

So Elizabeth went over to Kenneth and said, "I like your costume, Ken. You're a peddler, aren't you? How did you ever think of such a clever costume for a pioneer party?"

Kenneth explained that a story had given him the idea. Then Paul, Mrs. Willis' grandson, wanted to hear about the costume, too. Soon Kenneth and Elizabeth were feeling at home, laughing and talking with the other girls and boys.

64

"Oh, see the yellow-haired Indian!" Paul exclaimed, and all the children turned to see Jane coming in.

Now why had Jane dressed as an Indian girl for the pioneer party? To all the questions, Jane replied, "Ugh. Big secret. Guess."

But just then Mrs. Willis said, "Let's have a Spelling Bee and pretend you are real pioneer girls and boys in Williston's first schoolhouse. Allen and Elizabeth, will you be captains and choose teams?"

"Ken's a good speller. I'll take him," said Allen.

"I don't know about Paul's spelling," Elizabeth was thinking to herself, "but he'll feel queer if he's chosen last." So aloud she said, "I choose Paul."

The teams were soon ready and the Spelling Bee was on. The words became harder and harder until at last only Kenneth and one girl, Ann, were standing.

"Spell the word 'centennial,'" said Mrs. Willis.

"S-e-n-t-e-n-e-a-l," tried Ann. "No, that's wrong!"

"C-e-n-t-e-n-n-i-a-l," Kenneth spelled slowly.

"Right!" said Mrs. Willis. "Ken is the winner."

Everyone crowded around a smiling Kenneth as he unwrapped the prize—a model of a covered wagon.

What Mrs. Willis had planned to do next was quite different and a surprise. "I'm going to show you some early buildings in Williston," she said.

Mrs. Willis darkened the room and threw pictures on a screen—a log church, a general store, a cabin.

Allen looked hard at one picture of a plain white building and then asked, "Wasn't that a school?"

"Yes," Jane said, "Grandmother has that picture and it gave me the idea of dressing this way."

Paul was curious. "Go on, tell us why," he said.

"Well, Grandmother's mother, my great-grandmother," Jane explained, "went to that school. And next to her sat a little Indian girl, Mary White Cloud. They were good friends. That's why I wore an Indian dress—for Great-grandmother's friend."

"That *was* a good idea," said Mrs. Willis. "We haven't a prize for the cleverest costume, Jane, but you may be my special helper in getting the refreshments ready. And you may ask someone to help."

"I like that better than a prize," laughed Jane. "Come on, Elizabeth, you help me."

How busy Jane and Elizabeth were! They helped some children start popping corn. They put plates of sandwiches and cookies and glasses of apple cider on a table where the children could help themselves. And some of the girls helped Mrs. Willis make taffy candy for an old-fashioned taffy pull.

Nancy, Ann, and some of the others buttered their fingers and pulled the warm, sticky taffy until it was cool and golden.

Too soon the party was over and the children were saying good-bye.

"This party was tops," said Allen.

"I had such a good time," Jane said. "Thank you so much for everything, Mrs. Willis, and Paul, too."

"I didn't think a party could be so much fun," Kenneth told Mrs. Willis, and he added, "Paul, how about coming over to see me tomorrow? I live in the apartment house on the corner. We'd have fun."

"I'm *so* glad I was asked to come to this nice party," said Elizabeth. "And I'm so glad I met you, Paul. We had such a good time that I feel glad about everything! Oh, yes! I'm glad some people started this town a hundred years ago. If they hadn't, we wouldn't have had a party like this today! Good-bye."

Much to their surprise Kenneth and Elizabeth really enjoyed the party. What things helped change their opinions about parties?

How did Elizabeth help Kenneth feel more at ease? Notice that she complimented him on his costume.

A well-deserved compliment like this often makes another person feel happier and more at ease.

Notice that she also asked Kenneth a question. What was it? Elizabeth might merely have said, "What a clever costume!" But by asking a question, she made it easier for Kenneth to say something, too.

When you want a conversation to keep "moving along," ask a question now and then. The question gives the other person something to talk about and keeps him from feeling shy and wondering what to say next.

What else made Kenneth feel more at ease?

How did Kenneth and the others show they had enjoyed the party and had appreciated being asked?

Mrs. Willis' party was planned so that everyone could take part. Why was this good planning?

Would *you* like to have attended a party like this? Why or why not?

Did the party give you any ideas for planning one of your own? If so, what were they?

Things for You to Think About

1. It is often said that there is always a reason when your body does not act as it usually does.

What are some reasons why your heart might begin to beat faster? Why might you breathe faster? What are some other body changes that might result from worry or excitement?

2. Early in this unit you were promised that you would learn some ways of getting along better with yourself.

What have you learned that might help you when you are upset or out of sorts?

3. There are some good suggestions in this unit about ways of getting along better with others.

What are some of the suggestions?

4. Sam Jones doesn't like parties and doesn't want to go to them.

What suggestions could you give him to help him feel comfortable and make him enjoy going to parties?

5. Rose is discouraged because she skates poorly.

What suggestions might cheer her up?

6. When Jack's mother scolds about his appearance, he often says, "Nobody notices how I look!"

Is that really true? What are some occasions when people would be pretty sure to notice his looks?

7. Ella Wilson is hard to talk to. That is, she usually doesn't say much more than "yes" or "no" or "I think so" in conversations.

How might you make her feel at ease and help her talk more freely? What might Ella do to help herself be friendlier and more at ease?

8. One day the boys and girls in Sarah's class gave a program about "Our Bodies and How They Work."

Suppose you had been in this program. What might you have said about each of these topics?

The Digestive System   How We Breathe
The Work of the Heart   The Nervous System

9. Mary's music teacher wanted her to play in a piano recital, but Mary said, "I don't like to be in programs. I get too upset." So she stayed away.

Did she choose the best way to meet her problem of not liking to be in programs? What might have been a better way?

10. Dick was quarrelling with his older brother one day. At last he got so angry that he rushed out of the house. As he ran, he tripped and fell over a small branch of a tree that had blown down on the sidewalk. "I mustn't be so careless," he thought as he rubbed a bruised arm. "Next time I might get *really* hurt."

Did carelessness alone cause Dick's accident? What else might have caused it?

Things for You to Do

1. Using a watch, count the number of times you breathe in a minute. Did you find it was about 16 to 20 times? Would you expect this number to be the same for you at all times? Why or why not?

2. Now put two fingers of your right hand on the inside of your left wrist in line with your thumb and feel your *pulse*. Use a watch again and count the number of pulses or beats that your heart makes in a minute. Did you find it was about 80 to 90 beats a minute? When might it be more rapid than usual?

3. Plan and make a series of posters showing good ways of keeping your skin, hair, and nails clean.

4. Some of the class may enjoy making some cartoons showing "The Courteous Thing to Do or Say" for such occasions as arriving at or leaving a party or making a stranger welcome at school.

5. Some of the girls might enjoy trying different hair styles on each other. They might also try to discover which colors are most becoming. Pieces of colored paper or cloth might be held up to a girl's face to find which colors seem to look best.

6. Keep a record of the times when some part of your body behaves differently from the way it usually does. See if you can decide what the reason is.

You
and Your Family

CANADA'S
FOOD RULES

"Being the Oldest Girl Is No Fun!"

"Elizabeth, do this! Elizabeth, do that! Elizabeth, do the dishes! Elizabeth, watch the baby! Why doesn't anybody ever say 'Jo Ann, do something'?" grumbled Elizabeth one Saturday as she helped her mother in the kitchen. "All I do around here is *work*. It's no fun being the oldest girl in the family."

"Oh, come now, Elizabeth," said her mother. "It's not that bad. We'll be through with the re-frigerator soon, and you'll have all afternoon for whatever you want to do."

"But look at Jo Ann," Elizabeth said. "All *she* has to do is dry the dishes and dust a little."

"When you were her age, all *you* did was dry the dishes and dust a little," her mother reminded her. "But now that you are eleven, there are so many more things you can do. And you *are* a big help with the housework, Elizabeth. I wonder what I'd ever do without you."

"Maybe so," mumbled Elizabeth, even though she was secretly pleased at what her mother said. "Maybe so. But just the same I sometimes wish I were a boy like Ned and could help Dad at the store. Or I wish I were Jo Ann—or even Baby Meredith—and didn't have so much work to do."

"But there are advantages in being the oldest girl in the family," her mother said.

"Well, maybe there are," said Elizabeth, "but right now I can't seem to think of any."

Her mother smiled. "For one thing, you stay up later every night," she answered. "You know how Jo Ann argues, 'Why can't I stay up later—Elizabeth always does!'"

"You mean, you think that sometimes Jo Ann wishes she were my age?" asked Elizabeth.

"I'm sure she does," said her mother. "And don't forget that you have lots of other advantages. You get a bigger allowance, and——"

Just then the phone rang, and Mother answered it. "Hello. Oh, Mrs. Lee. Elizabeth? I'm sure she would like to very much. About two o'clock? Yes, I'll tell her, and if it isn't all right she'll call you back. She'd talk to you now, but she's up to her elbows in soapsuds! But I'm sure she will be delighted. Perhaps Jo Ann can go along, too."

75

Mother hung up the receiver and Elizabeth cried excitedly, "What did Mrs. Lee want, Mother?"

"Mrs. Lee's little niece is visiting her for the weekend. Mrs. Lee wants you to take her to the high school this afternoon to see 'Miraldo, the Wonder Magician,'" her mother answered.

"Oh, Mother," said Elizabeth. "Isn't that just wonderful! You know how much I wanted to see that show, but I'd spent all my allowance."

"Mrs. Lee said that she wanted someone a little older—and dependable," her mother smiled. "Someone she could trust to take care of her niece."

Elizabeth grinned, "I know what you're thinking, Mother. This is one of the advantages in being the oldest girl in the family."

Have you, like Elizabeth, ever been angry or upset because you thought others in the family had more privileges than you were allowed? When have you felt that way?

Elizabeth discovered that there are advantages as well as disadvantages in being the oldest girl in the family. What are some of the advantages?

If you ever find yourself fussing about being the oldest or the youngest or "the middle one," it will help to remember that *there are advantages as well as disadvantages in your particular place in the family.*

Everyone who lives in a family is likely to feel unfairly treated now and then. "My parents don't treat us all alike," you may occasionally complain. But if you stop to think, you will see that there are reasons why parents can't treat all their children in exactly the same way.

There is the matter of bedtime, for example. You know that younger children like Jo Ann need about twelve hours of sleep each night, while most boys and girls your age need about ten or eleven hours. That is why younger children must usually go to bed earlier. And that is just one example of why parents can't always treat all their children alike.

There is the matter of housework, too. It takes lots of work to keep a home running smoothly. It isn't fair to expect Mother to do all the work. Neither is it fair to expect the same amount of work from an eight-year-old as from a twelve-year-old child. Why not?

The fairest plan in a family is to have each one help according to his age and ability.

If you are an older child in the family, you can see that it is only fair that you help more than the younger children. It will make you feel better, too, to remember that your parents need and depend on you.

If you are a younger child and sometimes resent the privileges that older brothers and sisters have, it helps to realize that when you are older you will have these same privileges. It also helps if you do your work as well as you can and don't worry because you aren't quite so skilful as an older brother or sister. You'll improve with practice.

The pictures on page 79 show some situations that often occur in families. What is happening in Picture 1? Do *you* think it's fair that Henry but not Bob should make his own bed? Why or why not?

What advice would you give Carolyn, who is shown in Picture 2?

In Picture 3, Harriet seems to be upset. Why? Do you think her feelings are justified? What might she remember that would make her feel better?

In Picture 4, why do you think the boys' mother is not treating all of the boys alike? What should Jimmy remember that might cheer him up?

Do these situations remind you of anything that has happened in *your* family recently? What have you just learned that may help when you feel that others in the family are more favored than you?

HOMEMAKING

Elizabeth was impatient while waiting to go to the show that Saturday afternoon, so she decided to read her *Girl Guide Handbook* to help pass the time. As she looked through the "Homemaking" part, she was quite surprised.

"Why, I know about lots of the things in this chapter!" she thought. "I've learned about setting the table and making the table attractive just by helping Mother do it. And I've learned from her some of the very things this book tells about cooking and dishwashing."

And so it was that Elizabeth discovered another advantage in helping around the house—she was learning the kinds of things she would need to know when she grew up and had a home of her own.

For example, Elizabeth knew that the correct way to set each place at the table is the way shown below. Where are the napkin and the fork? Where are the knife and the spoon? The cup and saucer? The water glass? The bread-and-butter plate?

WHEN YOU EAT

"Meals taste better when the table looks pretty,"
Elizabeth's mother always says. So Elizabeth helps
by finding new ways to "fix up" the table.

What has Elizabeth used for the centrepiece on
the table shown in the picture above?

Here are some other
things that Elizabeth
sometimes uses for centre-
pieces. What are they?

What can *you* do to
make your dining table
look more attractive?

Which of the plates of food shown below look
the most appetizing to you? Why?

What other ways do you know that help make
food look attractive when it is being served?

81

When you eat your meals in pleasant surroundings, you are more likely to feel cheerful—and cheerful, happy feelings help you digest your food more easily. That is why pretty dining tables and attractively arranged platters of food are important. And that is why you should try to make mealtimes as pleasant as possible—and avoid quarrelling or getting upset at the table.

If you are unhappy or worried, it is a good plan to talk over your difficulties with your mother or father and try to do something about them *before* mealtimes. You will enjoy your meals much more if you can avoid being worried or upset when you come to the table. Your food will digest better, too, if you feel relaxed and at ease.

Your thoughts, as you have learned, affect the way your digestive system does its work. Further proof of this came not long ago when some scientists were able to see the stomach of a young man who had scalded his *esophagus,* or food tube, when he was a child. This young man had to be fed through a hole cut in his stomach.

The scientists noticed that when the young man was sad or afraid, the red wall of his stomach became pale—and his stomach did its work much more slowly than usual.

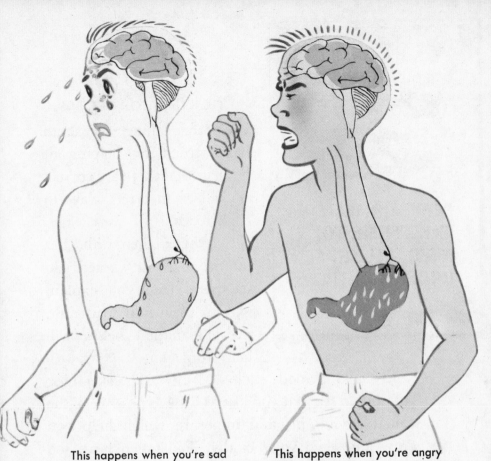

This happens when you're sad or afraid.

This happens when you're angry or excited.

When the young man was angry or excited, the red wall of his stomach became much redder. Extra digestive juices were produced in the stomach, even though very little food was in it. The stomach also *contracted*, or drew together, oftener than usual, and the young man was uncomfortable.

Now, how would you explain why it is important to have cheerful feelings when you eat?

Get the Good...
FROM YOUR FOOD

HEAT, AIR, WATER
TAKE THEIR TOLL
KEEP ALL THREE
UNDER CONTROL.

COOKING CORRECTLY

Another thing Elizabeth has learned by helping at home is that there are correct as well as incorrect ways to cook foods.

On the kitchen wall, her mother has the poster you see here. Can you explain what it means? If you can't, the explanation below will help you.

In cooking foods such as fruits and vegetables, you should see that you lose as little as possible of the valuable vitamins and minerals, which help you grow and keep you healthy. Too much heat, too much water, and too much "standing around" in the air can destroy these valuable vitamins and minerals.

Mashing potatoes or cooking them twice, as you do when you boil and then fry them, destroys most of the Vitamin C that is in them.

On page 85 are some other posters that tell about how to prepare fruits and vegetables. What is the reason for each suggestion?

Get the Good... FROM FRUIT

If fruit juice has to stand, keep covered and cold.

Cook in the peel if you can. If you must peel, make it thin.

2

Get the Good... FROM VEGETABLES

Wash quickly. Don't soak.

Keep cool. Keep in Nature's covering until ready to cook.

Cut just before using.

3

Get the Good... FROM VEGETABLES

Cook in boiling water, with no more than needed.

Watch the clock. Cook quickly. Stop when tender.

Don't use soda. It destroys the vitamins.

Serve in its own juice. Save the juice for sauce or soup or gravy.

4

Get the Good... FROM VEGETABLES

Boiled or baked, Nature's jacket holds in the good.

Heat canned foods quickly. They're already cooked. Use all the juices.

Start cooking frozen vegetables while still frozen. Don't thaw first.

5

THE SAFE WAY TO DO DISHES

Elizabeth has also learned a good way to wash dishes—a way that uses plenty of soap and hot water to help destroy any harmful germs that may be on the dishes or silverware.

The pictures below show the way to wash dishes safely. What is happening in each picture?

What have *you* learned from these pictures that will help you the next time you wash dishes?

The dishes are scraped with a rubber scraper or some soft paper.

The dishes are stacked in neat piles, and the silverware is put in one place.

Cooking dishes are put to soak in cold water, and greasy pots and pans are put to soak in warm, soapy water.

The dishpan or sink is filled with hot, soapy water. If necessary, it is later emptied and then refilled with more clean, hot, soapy water.

The glasses are washed first, then the silverware, then the dishes, and last of all the pots and pans.

Boiling water is poured over the dishes and silverware that are stacked in the drainer. The dishes and silverware are left to dry in the drainer, or they are dried with clean dish towels.

In handling the dishes and silverware, either when setting the table or when putting them away, Elizabeth has learned to carry them in a way that helps keep from spreading germs from her hands to the clean utensils.

Which pictures below show Elizabeth's way—*the correct way*—of handling dishes and silverware?

What is wrong in the other pictures?

What have *you* learned from these pictures that will remind you of correct ways to handle dishes and other eating utensils?

THIS ➡

THIS ➡

THIS ➡

Wear rubber-soled shoes when you are standing on a damp floor and using a washing machine.

KEEPING SAFE AT HOME

Elizabeth has learned, too, through helping around the house to be very careful with *electrical equipment.*

"Never touch any piece of electrical equipment with wet hands," her mother often reminds her. "If you are wiping off the toaster with a damp cloth, be sure to pull the cord out of the socket first. And always be sure that your hands are dry when you plug in the cord for the iron or when you turn on a switch in the electric stove."

Keep electrical equipment in good repair . . .

Put a cord or plastic chain on the metal chain . . . Don't touch a metal chain-pull with wet hands.

Watch for frayed cords and get them fixed.

REMEMBER

DON'T TOUCH ELECTRICAL EQUIPMENT

You, too, must learn to be very careful with the electrical equipment in your home. One thing you must always remember is that *when your body is wet it is easier for an electric current to enter your body through the skin and give you an electric shock.*

That is why you should never touch any electrical equipment when you have wet hands or when you are in the bathtub or standing on a damp floor.

What other safety precautions are suggested in the pictures on this page and on page 88?

Pull out cords by the safety handles.

Keep young children away from electrical equipment.

Keep electric heaters away from the bathtub.

WITH WET HANDS.

What Do You Think?

1. When Edward's class was talking about correct ways to wash dishes, Edward said, "I'm not interested in things like that. Boys and men don't need to know those things. Doing dishes is women's work!"

Do you agree that "doing dishes is women's work"? What are some reasons why brothers or fathers are often needed to help with such work as doing dishes?

2. One day Sam saw his mother pouring the water in which potatoes had been cooked into the pan where she was going to make gravy. "Why are you doing that?" he asked. "Why don't you throw that old water away?"

How would you answer Sam's questions?

3. "Sally Freedman never has to do any work at home," said Jane. "Her mother and the maid do all the work. Don't you think Sally's awfully lucky?"

Do you think Sally is "awfully lucky"? What makes you think as you do?

4. One morning little Jo Ann set the table. This picture shows how she set one place.

Would you call Jo Ann "a good table setter"? What hints could you give her about setting a table?

90

"You Like *Him* Better!"

"Where's my violin?" cried Larry. "I tell you I have to have it, Allen! Where did you hide it?"

"What did you say?" asked Allen. "I was busy reading, and I didn't hear you."

"You heard me all right," exclaimed Larry. "You hid that violin and you know you did. And you'd just better tell me where it is. You'll be sorry if you don't."

"Allen!" said his mother, who had come into the room as Larry was speaking. "Have you been teasing your brother again?"

"He hid my violin," said Larry. "And I have to have it. I have to practise some more before my lesson this afternoon."

"Allen," said his mother. "Go find that violin and bring it here this minute!"

"Oh, all right, I'll get it," said Allen. "I was only fooling and Larry ought to know it."

So Allen "found" the violin, and soon Larry was busy practising. And Allen was busy talking things over with his mother.

"*Why* do you tease Larry so much?" Mother asked. "There's just no peace around here lately, the way you've been quarrelling with your brother."

"Why blame *me* for all the quarrelling?" grumbled Allen. "You never blame Larry. You think Larry's wonderful. I heard you talking over the phone the other day and telling some lady how proud you were of him. You said he's going to be the youngest one to play in the big music recital at the high school next week. I think you like him better than you do me, that's what I think!"

"Why, Allen, of course I don't," answered his mother. "I am proud of the way Larry is learning to play the violin. But I am just as proud of you for other things, and so is your Dad. We never fail to show our guests the bookcases and the many other things you made in your workshop. We're proud of your work."

Then his mother went on to say, "Now I begin to see what's been troubling you lately, Allen. You have the mistaken idea that I love Larry more than I love you. That's been making you unhappy, and you've been taking out some of your feelings on Larry. Don't you think that may be your trouble?"

"Well-ll," said Allen, "I hadn't thought about it that way before. But I guess I did wonder if you were prouder of Larry than of me. I didn't think about your being proud of the things I could do. I was too busy thinking about Larry and the way you let him go to Lake City on the bus every Saturday— all by himself. You even let him eat lunch in the cafeteria over there sometimes."

"You could do those things, too," his mother pointed out. "But you don't want to go over to Lake City for music lessons. You've told us that often. And you forget that part of the time when you are playing with your friends, Larry is busy practising."

"That's so," admitted Allen. "I'd hate to do all the practising he does."

"And this afternoon," his mother reminded him, "while Larry is in Lake City taking his music lesson, you'll be at the high school enjoying the magician's show with the other boys and girls."

"Say!" cried Allen. "I'd almost forgotten about that. I certainly wouldn't want to be Larry today. I'd much rather be ME!"

Like Allen, you may sometimes feel that your mother and father like a brother or sister more than they like you. Perhaps an older brother is chosen for the basketball team and your father is so proud he tells all the neighbors about it. A sister may bring home a report card that is much better than yours. Or one of your sisters may begin to take music lessons or dancing lessons because she seems to have special talent or ability.

At times like these it is easy to see how you might feel a little left out of things, or even feel that your parents must be fonder and prouder of a brother or sister than of you.

Such feelings are rather common. You may begin to worry because you think you aren't so athletic or so bright or so talented as one of the others in the family. You may even begin to feel angry at your brother or sister. Without quite realizing what you are doing, you may "take out" your feelings on your brother or sister, as Allen "took out" his feelings on Larry by teasing him. You may brag about what you can do and make fun of what your brother or sister has done. Or you may become too "bossy" or too much of a bully.

If you find yourself getting into the habit of teasing, bullying, "bossing," or bragging to a brother or sister, you should stop and think, "What is making me act this way?"

Once you understand and admit that you may be jealous of a brother or sister, you can do something about your feelings.

For example, you can remind yourself that *each one in a family is an individual. That is, each one is different and has a different appearance, different talents, and different weaknesses—and it's these differences that make life more fun!*

You can also try to remember that *few of us do everything equally well*—and that *although your brother or sister may do some things better than you, there are other things in which you excel.*

You will feel better, as Allen did, when you realize that your parents are just as proud of what you can do as of what your brothers and sisters can do. Your parents know that it wouldn't be very interesting if all the children in the family looked alike, acted alike, and had just exactly the same talents. That's why you often hear mothers and fathers say, "One of the most fascinating things about being parents is that no matter how many children you have, each one is different from all the others!"

Now look at the picture at the left below and see if you can explain why Sue is acting as she is. Will her actions be likely to make her happier or change the situation she does not like? How might she help change her feelings to more pleasant ones?

Look at the picture at the right below. Is Bess handling her disappointment in a more helpful way than Sue? Why or why not?

Have you ever "taken out" your feelings on your brother or sister? What did you do? What made you act that way? What might you have done instead?

What have you just learned that will help you next time you feel jealous of a brother or sister?

Anybody could be in a little old play like yours. I bet nobody will even come to see it. I wouldn't be in a play like that. When I'm in high school, though, I'll be in a real play, with fancy costumes and everything.

I wish I had been chosen to be in the school play. But anyway, I'm glad you were chosen, Tom. It will be fun to have someone in the family in it. And maybe I'll be in something soon. I'm going to try out for the Girl's Glee Club this spring.

DO YOU KNOW HOW TO RELAX?

After lunch on Saturday, Larry and Allen helped their mother with the dishes. Then Larry said, "I have an hour before I take the bus for Lake City. I think I'll practise some more on my violin."

"Oh, Larry," said his mother, "why don't you take it easy for a while? You practised a long time this morning. I'm afraid you work too hard at your music. And when you play, you play too hard. You'll have to learn to take it easy now and then."

"Like me," said Allen, who was stretched out on the davenport. "I'm going to stay here and listen to the football game on the radio until it's time to go to the magician's show this afternoon."

Larry's mother was right in her advice to Larry. We all feel better when we rest a bit, or *relax*, after a meal or between periods of hard work or play.

A little rest after a meal gives your stomach a better chance to digest your food. And short periods of rest and relaxing now and then during the day or a short nap, if things have been pretty strenuous, will keep you from getting overtired and cross.

When you read about the heart on page 33, you learned another reason for resting between periods of hard work or active games. What is the reason?

You not only feel better but you can usually work better if you stop to rest or relax now and then. For example, if you are playing ball or cleaning the basement or working on a model airplane, you may be tempted to overwork or to keep going steadily until the job is done. But if you do this, you may find you won't get as much or as good work done as you would if you took a little time out to rest. When you get over-tired, your muscles don't work so well and you don't accomplish so much. To make your muscles work well again, you must stop and rest a little.

Allen had learned one good way to relax after a meal. What was it?

The pictures below show some other good ways of relaxing occasionally. What are they?

What is your favorite way of relaxing?

WHAT'S YOUR HOBBY?

Allen had a hobby that gave him much pleasure. What was his hobby?

His friends had some interesting hobbies, too. The pictures below show some of their hobbies. What are they?

Perhaps *you* have a hobby that you enjoy. What is your hobby? How did you happen to become interested in it? Why do you think others might enjoy your hobby, too?

Like Allen, you may have a hobby that has kept you interested for months or longer. On the other hand, you may change your interests and your hobbies quite often. Lots of boys and girls your age do that. So don't feel guilty because you start building a model plane or making a puppet show and then get bored and turn to other things before you finish. *A hobby is something you do just for fun. It's no longer a hobby when you do it because you think you ought to!*

Maybe you haven't a hobby and you wonder, "What's the use of a hobby anyway?" The pictures below show that life is often more interesting to those who have hobbies. Which boy and which girl have hobbies? What makes you think so?

Of course, even a hobby can be "too much of a good thing." That is, you may work too hard on your hobby, or you may spend so much time on it that you don't get the *hour or two hours of outdoor play and exercise you need each day.*

Joe Wilson, for example, has become so interested in his new Builder Set that he wants to work with it every afternoon after school until suppertime.

Joe needs to learn to plan his time so that he can get the outdoor play he needs and still have time for his Builder Set. When might Joe work on his hobby?

Another time a hobby can become "too much of a good thing" is when so much time is spent on it that little time is left for friends. This may happen especially to children who have trouble making friends.

Edith Howe, for example, finds it difficult to make friends. So she has begun to spend too much time with books, instead of with boys and girls her own age. What Edith needs to do is to spend less time with her hobby and more time trying to make friends.

For one thing, Edith might invite one or two of the girls in her class to come home and play with her after school. Or she might notice which girls in her class also like to read very much and then talk over with them some of her favorite books. What are some other things she might do to be friendly?

All about Yourself

Here are some questions that will help you make an interesting record about yourself. The questions will also help your teacher know more about you—and more about your family, your friends, your favorite activities, and your feelings about certain things. Your teacher will tell you how she wants you to copy this record and fill in your answers.

I. *Your Family*

    1. What work does your father do?_____

    2. Does your mother work?_____

    3. What are the names and ages of the other children in your family?_____

    4. Do both parents live at home?_____

    5. Have you any special troubles or problems in getting along with others in your family?

    _____

II. *Your Friends*

    1. If your mother said you might invite a classmate for dinner, who would it be?_____

    2. If this boy or girl couldn't come, whom would you ask?_____

    3. Suppose the second person couldn't come, whom would you ask?_____

4. Suppose you needed help with your arithmetic and the teacher told you to ask a friend for help, whom would you ask?_____

5. If you were working on a science exhibit, whom would you want to help you?_____

6. Write the name of the boy in your class who you think gets along best with his classmates.

   _____

7. Write the name of the girl in your class who you think gets along best with her classmates.

   _____

III. *Your Hobbies and Other Activities*

1. What do you usually do:
   directly after school?_____
   in the evenings?_____
   on Saturdays?_____

2. If you have been to any of these places, underline them.

   a farm   a concert
   a circus   an opera
   a zoo   a stage play
   an art museum   a summer camp
   an amusement park   a radio station

3. How often do you go to the movies?_____

4. What are the names of two of the best moving pictures you have ever seen?_____

5. Do you take music lessons or other special lessons?_____If so, what kind?_____
6. What are your favorite radio programs?____

_____
7. What chores do you do regularly at home?

_____
8. Have you a hobby?_____
If so, what?_____
9. Have you a library card?_____What are some good books you have read lately?

_____
10. What magazines do you often read?_____

_____
11. Have you a pet?_____What?_____

IV. *Your Feelings*
1. Do you enjoy spending time at home?_____
Why or why not?_____
2. Do you like school?_____Why or why not?_____
3. If you had three wishes that might come true, what would they be?_____

_____
4. What things do you often wonder about?

_____
5. What things do you sometimes worry about?

_____

What Do You Think?

1. The children in Helen's family agreed to clean up the basement if they could have a Harvest Party there later. Jean wanted to do all the work one day after school, but Dick thought they ought to wait until Saturday when they'd have more time and wouldn't get so tired.

Which plan do you think was the better one? Why?

2. One morning Gretchen discovered that her sister Mary had borrowed her ice skates without asking her. Gretchen was very angry, but she thought, "I won't say anything until dinnertime. Then I'll tell Mary what I think about her! Maybe Dad will scold her when he hears about what she did."

Do you think Gretchen picked the best time for fussing about the skates? Why or why not?

3. One day the doorknob on the kitchen door came off, and Mrs. Nicola thought she would have to have a repairman come to fix it. But her son Victor said, "I can fix it." And he did.

"Thanks, Victor!" said his mother. "I should have known you could fix it. You're *so* handy."

"Hm!" thought Victor's younger brother Joe. "Mother never says anything like that about me!

I'll bet she'd miss Victor a lot if he weren't here. But she wouldn't miss me much."

What might Joe have kept in mind when he began to think his mother liked Victor more than she liked him?

4. Many stores and factories have their workers take one or two short rest periods during the day.

Why is that a good rule for the workers? Might the rule help the stores and factories, too? How?

5. From the time she was very small, Cathie had been interested in the piano. When she was six, her parents decided that she should have piano lessons. Her older sister June wasn't really interested in music, but she said, "If Cathie takes lessons, I want to take them, too."

Do you think June should insist that she have music lessons, too? Why might it be fair for Cathie but not June to have the lessons?

6. "It's all very well to say most parents are as fond of one child as of another," complained Dan. "But in *our* family that isn't true. Betty's the only girl and she's the baby, too! She gets anything she wants."

"Oh," said Henry, "you're just imagining things! What do you want that you don't get? I'll bet Betty isn't treated any differently from the way you were treated when you were the baby."

What do you think of Henry's answer to Dan?

106

"Why Can't I?"

"But Mother, why can't I go?" exclaimed Kenneth. "I only have a little sniffle, and staying just one night at the Boy Scout Cabin can't hurt me."

"Ken, I've told you over and over that it wouldn't be safe. You'd be sure to get chilled and make your cold worse. Anyway, it wouldn't be fair to the other boys for you to go. You might give them your cold, you know."

"Oh, Mother!" cried Kenneth. "Please let me go. This is the first time I've had the chance. I just passed my Tenderfoot Test a week ago. Please let me call the Scoutmaster and tell him I can go after all. He has to know by ten o'clock. If I don't call him by then, it'll be too late."

107

"I'm sorry, Ken," said his mother. "I don't like to see you disappointed. But when you have a cold, home is the best place——"

Ken jumped up, interrupting his mother, "I've just got to go, Mother, I've just got to! I'm going to talk to Dad!" And he ran out of the room and down into the basement where his father was working.

"Dad," he said, almost in tears, "you don't want the fellows to think I'm a sissy, do you? Can't you persuade Mother to let me go on the hike?"

"No, Ken," said his father. "Your mother and I talked it over early this morning. It's too bad about your cold, but since you have it, the best thing for you to do is to stay home."

"It's not fair!" cried Kenneth. "I never have any fun like the other fellows do. You treat me like a baby. So I'll just be one. I'll just sit in my room all day, that's what I'll do." And with that Kenneth ran up to his room and slammed the door.

But his father followed him to his room. "Listen, Ken," he said, "I know how you feel, but acting this way won't help. Taking disappointments is part of learning how to be a man. And there'll be other hikes, you know."

Just then Mother appeared at the door. "Kenneth, you left before I finished talking with you. I wanted to remind you that there are some things you can do at home today to have fun."

Ken's face brightened a little. "What things can I do?" he asked.

"Well, you can listen with me to the football game on the radio this afternoon," said his father.

"And you can help me learn how to use the new pressure cooker," his mother said. "Didn't you say your Scout troop was going to do some cooking this weekend? This recipe book tells about some one-dish stews that you might practise on——"

"Say," said Ken, "that's a pretty good idea. The fellows are going to learn to cook a 'Hunter's Stew' outdoors tonight for their supper. Is there a recipe for that? If I can't be with the others at the cabin tonight, I can still learn to make a stew, can't I?"

Daddy promised to take me to the Motor Show this afternoon, and I don't care if he does have to work overtime. He ought to leave work early and take me, just as he said he would. And I'm going to tell him that when he gets home.

You mean I can't have a new dress for the party—after I've been counting on it all this time? Oh, well, if I can't, I can't! Could we buy some new trimming for my old party dress?

Look at that storm! Now we can't have our Model Plane Flying Contest today. I might as well go back to bed and sleep the rest of the morning. My day is spoiled anyhow!

WHEN DISAPPOINTMENTS COME

Kenneth was quite disappointed because he couldn't go on the hike with the other Boy Scouts. His disappointment was so great that at first he wanted to do nothing but stay in his own room. Later, after listening to his father's advice and talking to his mother, he found a better way of handling his disappointment. What was this way?

Sulking, of course, is one way of behaving when you are disappointed. The pictures above show some other ways boys and girls have of meeting disappointments. What is happening in each picture?

Which children are probably making themselves more unhappy by the way they are acting? Which one is trying to find a way to "make the best" of the situation?

Now and then you, too, will have disappointments of one kind or another. You may have to stay home to tend the baby instead of playing with your friends. Your parents may refuse to give you permission to do something that all your friends are planning to do.

At times like these you may feel very upset or angry or unhappy. You may do some grumbling. But if you are wise, you won't spoil your day by continued grumbling, sulking, crying, or temper tantrums. These ways of behaving don't change matters, anyway.

The best way of meeting a disappointment is to accept it and then see if you can't make some other plans or find some other way of enjoying yourself.

We all have occasional disappointments. And while they may seem hard or unfair, we must all learn to accept certain things and adjust to them.

Now look at the pictures on page 110 again. What might the girl in the picture at the left decide to do instead of crying and grumbling? What might the boy in the middle picture do instead of having a temper tantrum? Are their actions helping the situations that they don't like or are fussing over?

What big disappointment have *you* had recently? How did you act about it? Would you act that way if you had it to do over again? Why or why not?

Sometimes the hardest part of a disappointment comes when you have to explain to your friends why you can't do what you had planned to do.

Kenneth, you will remember, said, "You don't want the fellows to think I'm a sissy, do you?" Kenneth knew that when he saw his friends, he would have to face the problem of explaining why he couldn't go on the hike.

The pictures below show three ways he might have used in explaining this situation to his friends. Which way do you think is the most satisfactory? How might Kenneth's actions in the first two pictures influence the way the other boys feel toward him?

How would you justify this advice?—*"When you have to explain a disappointment to others, it is best to tell frankly why you can't do what you had planned to do."*

If you have a cold, it is not wise to go on a hike. Why not?

Boy Scouts, and Girl Guides too, are very careful in planning hikes so that they will be safe and healthful. Ken's parents know that, and they will probably be very willing to let him go on a hike the next time, provided he hasn't a cold.

Do you know about the care that Scouts take when they go on a hike? Each Scout, for example, is expected to have certain clothing for hikes. Why do you think he is told to have the following things?

Comfortable shoes—sturdy, and not "too new"

Thick socks or stockings, woollen if possible

Loose, comfortable clothing—enough to keep him warm while walking and something woollen to use when he is sitting around resting

A raincoat or slicker in case of rain

On the hike itself, Boy Scouts always take care to observe safety precautions. If you study the picture map on page 115, you can follow the route that the Scouts in Kenneth's troop took to their cabin.

What safety precaution did the boys take as they walked along the highway? Why is this important?

What did the boys do to make sure they would have no accidents at the railway crossing?

To make sure they had pure water to drink the boys carried canteens filled with safe drinking water. Why isn't it safe to drink from "just any" stream or well you may pass?

From which places shown in the pictures above would you feel it is safe to drink water? Why?

If you aren't sure you will find pure drinking water on a hike, it is a good plan to take along some water in a container as the Scouts did in their canteens. Or you can boil water to make it safe to drink.

Another precaution the Scouts took was to stay away from the poison ivy they saw growing here and there along the roadway. Since it was late fall, most of the leaves had dropped off these plants. But the Scouts had been taught not to go near poison ivy, poison oak, or poison sumac *at any time of the year* because both the leaves and the *vines* are poisonous.

The Scouts also learned to recognize the poisonous plants shown below. And that is a good thing for you to do, too. This little verse will help you know them— and will remind you to stay away from them:

Leaves three,
Quickly flee!
Berries white,
Take flight!

Poison ivy

Poison oak

Poison sumac

WHEN FIRST AID IS NEEDED

Another piece of equipment that Boy Scouts and Girl Guides take along on hikes is shown in the little picture at the left. What is it? Why might it be useful at home as well?

Something most Boy Scouts and Girl Guides learn is how to give *first aid*, or immediate care, to slight injuries. Later they learn about giving first aid to badly injured persons while waiting for a doctor to come.

The pictures below and on the next two pages show what they learn to do in case of *nosebleed, stomach ache, pimple on the face, cinder in the eye, insect bites, frostbite*, and *poison ivy.*

Study these pictures until *you* know the correct first-aid treatment for each of these injuries. Then plan a first-aid quiz to be used in your class.

WHAT TO DO FOR A NOSEBLEED

Apply cold wet cloths over the nose.

Sit with head slightly back. Loosen the collar.

Pinch the nostrils for about five minutes. If bleeding doesn't sto[p] see a doctor.

WHAT TO DO FOR A STOMACH ACHE

Use no medicine!
Because stomach pain may be a
sign of appendicitis, the best thing to do if
the pain continues is to call a doctor. In the
meantime, the patient should rest in bed without taking any food or any laxative until the
doctor arrives.

WHAT TO DO FOR A PIMPLE

The safest thing to do about a pimple is to let it
alone! Or apply a little rubbing alcohol to help
it dry up.
Never squeeze a pimple. The squeezing of
pimples may cause serious infections.
If you have a lot of trouble with pimples, ask
your family doctor about what to do. Don't use
any medicine unless he tells you to.

WHAT TO DO FOR A CINDER IN THE EYE

Wait for a few minutes
to see if a flow of
tears will wash out
the cinder or bit of
dirt.

Gently grasp the
lashes of the upper
lid and pull it out
and down over the
lower lid.
Do not rub the eye!

Try washing out the
eye with sterile
water, which is
water that has been
boiled and then
cooled.

If these methods do not help, you should see a doctor.

WHAT TO DO FOR AN INSECT BITE

Remove the "sting" if it is in the bite.

Apply clean cloths moistened with ammonia water, or apply thick paste of baking soda.

WHAT TO DO FOR FROSTBITE

Get out of the wind as quickly as possible.

Bring the injured part into contact with some other part of the body. For example, place the open hands over frostbitten face or ears.

Apply cloths wrung out of cool water. Slowly raise the temperature of the water until it is lukewarm. Do not put snow on a frostbite!

WHAT TO DO FOR POISON OAK, POISON IVY, AND POISON SUMAC

Learn to recognize these poisonous plants so you can avoid them.

But if you think you have been in contact with any of these plants, take a thorough bath, using yellow laundry soap if possible, and put on clean underwear. Also change and wash your outer clothing since some of the poison may be left on it.

If a rash appears, it is a good plan to see a doctor. He will recommend a calamine lotion or some other medicine that will give you relief.

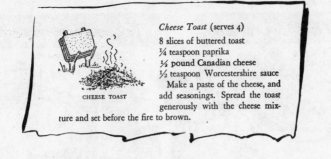

Cheese Toast (serves 4)

8 slices of buttered toast
¼ teaspoon paprika
⅓ pound Canadian cheese
½ teaspoon Worcestershire sauce

Make a paste of the cheese, and add seasonings. Spread the toast generously with the cheese mixture and set before the fire to brown.

CHEESE TOAST

THE FOODS YOU NEED

The Scouts in Kenneth's troop enjoyed learning to plan and cook meals. One recipe they liked is shown above. Boy Scout and Girl Guide leaders, you know, are careful to plan balanced meals on trips and at camps—meals that contain foods important for good health.

The kinds of foods we all need are described below and on pages 120 to 125.

FOODS FOR GROWTH AND HEALTH

Have you ever stopped to think how much you have grown since you were a tiny baby, weighing six or eight pounds? The material for all this growth has come from the foods you eat.

As you use your body every day, different parts of it wear out. These tiny parts or *cells* must be repaired when they wear out. The material for this repair must come from the foods you eat.

One material that helps your body grow and that keeps it repaired comes from foods containing *protein*.

119

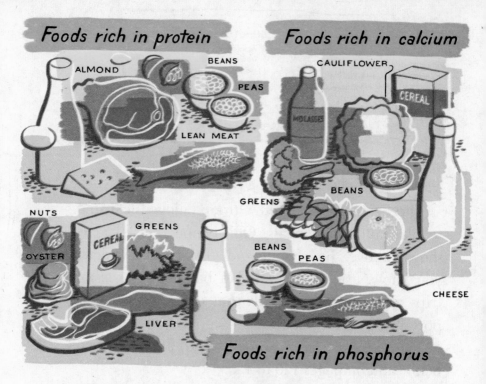

Foods rich in protein

ALMOND
BEANS
PEAS
LEAN MEAT

Foods rich in calcium

CAULIFLOWER
CEREAL
MOLASSES
BEANS
GREENS

NUTS
GREENS
CEREAL
OYSTER
BEANS
PEAS
CHEESE
LIVER

Foods rich in phosphorus

Protein foods not only help you grow, but they give you pep for work and play. Notice the important protein foods in the picture above.

But protein foods are not the only ones you need to help you grow and to keep you healthy. You also need foods with minerals called *calcium* and *phosphorus*. Foods with calcium and phosphorus in them are especially valuable in helping to build strong bones and teeth. The foods that are richest in calcium are milk and cheese. We get phosphorus in so many of our foods that we don't need to worry about getting enough of it.

You need other minerals besides calcium and phosphorus to keep your body healthy. There are about fourteen different minerals you need, but you get most of them without having to think especially about them. However, you need to choose your food well to get enough of the mineral *iron*.

Foods that have iron in them help keep your blood healthy. In the picture below you see some of the foods from which people get the iron they need. What are they?

Your body needs only a little iodine, but it needs that little bit very much. You get iodine if you eat plenty of food from the ocean—fish, oysters, clams, and other seafoods. To make sure that we in Canada get enough of this important mineral, all our table salt now contains iodine. It says so on the box. When you go home today, take a look at the box of salt in your cupboard to see that this is so.

Foods rich in iron

ALMOND
BEANS
PEAS
RAISINS
LIVER
OATMEAL
OYSTER
EGG YOLKS
DRIED FRUIT
BROWN RICE

The picture on page 123 shows some foods that are rich in vitamins. Here are some of the things that the vitamins in these foods can do for you.

Vitamin A helps you grow well and have healthy skin, eyes, and teeth. It keeps the linings of your mouth and throat healthy and helps protect them from disease.

Vitamin B is not just one vitamin but a group of vitamins, called vitamin B_1, B_2, and so on. This group of vitamins as a whole helps you digest your food, helps make good blood, and keeps your skin and nerves in good condition.

Vitamin C helps keep your teeth and gums healthy.

Vitamin D helps your body use the calcium and phosphorus in foods for building bones and teeth. Vitamin D is sometimes called *the sunshine vitamin* because your body makes this vitamin for itself when summer sunlight shines on the skin. But in winter you do not get as much sunlight as you need, because you wear more clothes, because there is less sunshine, and because smoke often shuts off the sunshine.

In winter it is a good plan to take cod-liver oil or other fish-liver oil or vitamin-D milk to get the extra vitamin D your body needs.

SPINACH

CARROTS

BUTTER

MARGARINE
VITAMIN A

LIVER

EGG YOLKS

Foods rich in vitamin A

CEREAL
WHOLE GRAIN

WHOLE WHEAT BREAD

WHEAT GERM

DRIED BEANS PEAS

LIVER

GREENS

PORK SOYBEANS

Foods rich in vitamin B

STRAW-BERRIES

MELON

PEPPER

GRAPE-FRUIT

ORANGE

BRUSSELS SPROUTS

BROCCOLI

LEMON

TOMATO

Foods rich in vitamin C

123

VITAMIN D MILK

COD LIVER OIL TABLETS

HALIBUT LIVER OIL TABLETS

Foods rich in vitamin D

FOODS FOR WARMTH AND ENERGY

The temperature of your body, as you know, stays just about the same all the time. Even when you go outside in cold weather, your body keeps warm on the inside. That is because heat is made inside your body to keep it warm. This heat comes from the foods you eat.

Some of the foods you eat are called fuel or energy foods. These foods burn inside your body. As they are burned, heat is made—and this heat keeps your body warm and gives you energy to move about and to work and play.

You get energy from every kind of food except salt, but the two most important groups of foods that give you heat and energy are called *fats* and *carbohydrates*. Butter, lard, and margarine may be the fat foods that you know best. You can see these and other fat foods in the picture below. What are they?

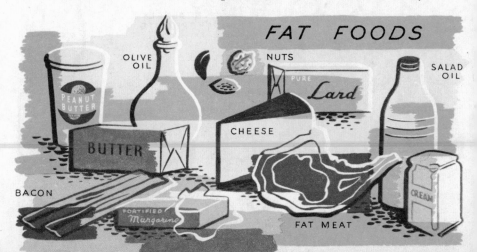

FAT FOODS

OLIVE OIL · NUTS · SALAD OIL · PEANUT BUTTER · PURE Lard · BUTTER · CHEESE · CREAM · BACON · FORTIFIED Margarine · FAT MEAT

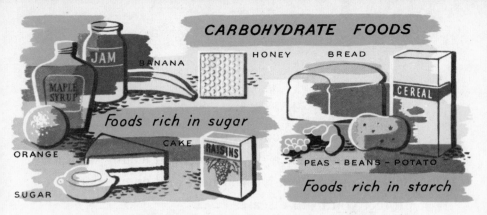

Foods rich in sugar

Foods rich in starch

JAM

MAPLE SYRUP

BANANA

HONEY

BREAD

CEREAL

ORANGE

CAKE

RAISINS

PEAS - BEANS - POTATO

SUGAR

Carbohydrate foods are those with starch and sugar in them. You can easily tell when you are eating sugar or a food with sugar in it. Any food with a sweet taste has sugar in it. Most fruits and a few vegetables have some sugar in them.

Foods with lots of sugar in them, such as candy, doughnuts, and cakes, satisfy your hunger. But if you eat these foods between meals, they may spoil your appetite for other foods you need. That is why you should avoid eating many sweet foods between meals.

Foods with lots of starch in them are bread, potatoes, cereal, peas, and beans. You need some of these foods every day as well as some foods with fat and sugar in them.

The amount of fat and carbohydrate foods you need each day depends partly on the weather but more on the energy you are using. Why do you need more of these foods in winter? Why do you need more of them when you play hard outdoors than when you play quietly indoors?

125

You have learned about the different kinds of foods you need each day to keep you feeling well, to help you grow, to give you heat and energy, and to protect you from disease.

Maybe you have noticed, too, that the foods you eat have a great deal to do with the way you feel. When you have eaten too much, you often feel lazy. You move slowly and don't want to play.

When you haven't had enough to eat, or enough of the right kinds of food, you may be cross or fussy or have very little pep. Knowing about the different foods and what they do is important for lots of reasons, you see.

Of course, it isn't enough just to know what these foods are. You also need to learn to plan your diet so that you will be sure to eat enough of the right kinds of food every day. The chart on page 127 shows an easy way to plan your diet to include these foods. Study this chart until you know what the important foods are.

You will notice that tea and coffee are not included in any of these groups. That is because tea and coffee have no food value and are not good for growing girls and boys. It is better to drink milk instead.

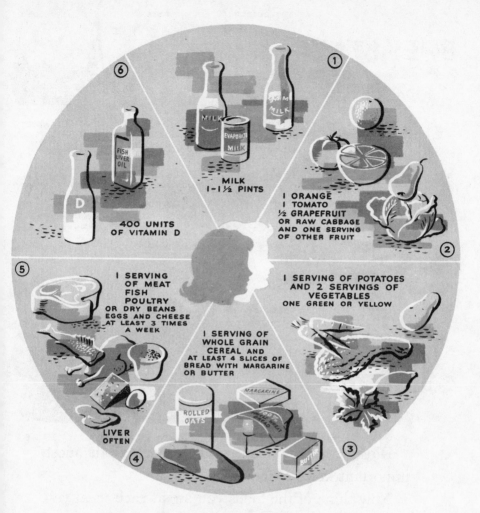

EAT THESE FOODS EVERY DAY

Now look at the picture at the top of page 128. This picture shows the menu that the Scouts in Kenneth's troop had on the Sunday they spent at the Boy Scout Cabin. Check this menu with the chart at the top of this page.

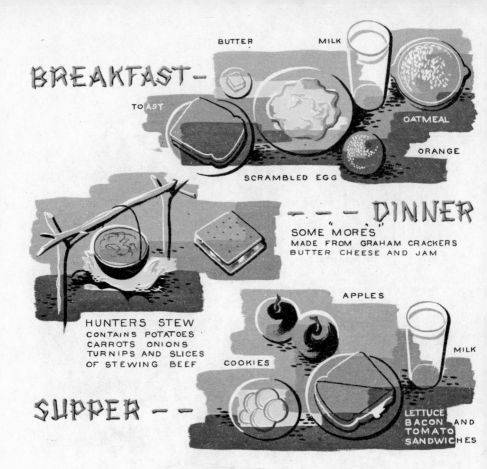

BREAKFAST—

BUTTER MILK

TOAST

OATMEAL

ORANGE

SCRAMBLED EGG

— — — DINNER

SOME "MORES"
MADE FROM GRAHAM CRACKERS
BUTTER CHEESE AND JAM

HUNTERS STEW
CONTAINS POTATOES
CARROTS ONIONS
TURNIPS AND SLICES
OF STEWING BEEF

APPLES

MILK

COOKIES

SUPPER — —

LETTUCE
BACON AND
TOMATO
SANDWICHES

Did the Scouts include in their meals all the most important kinds of food?

Now think of the foods you ate at each meal yesterday. On a piece of paper draw lines for three columns. At the top of the first column write *Breakfast,* at the top of the second write *Lunch,* and at the top of the third write *Dinner.* Or if you have your heavy meal at noon, write *Dinner* at the top of the second column, and *Supper* at the top of the third.

128

Now in the columns write what you ate at each meal. Then check with the chart on page 127. Did you eat enough of the foods from each group? If not, what foods should you have added to your diet yesterday?

Look at the foods in the picture below. Use these foods to help you make out a menu for breakfast, lunch, and dinner. If you carry your lunch, plan a balanced menu for it. Be sure every menu includes some food from each of the important food groups.

Beverages
CREAMED SOUP
MILK
ORANGE JUICE

STEWED APRICOTS
APPLE
Fruits
SLICED BANANAS
GRAPE-FRUIT
SLICED ORANGES

Vegetables
BAKED POTATO
GREEN BEANS
CARROTS
ASPARAGUS
SQUASH
CABBAGE SLAW

VITAMIN A MARGARINE
BUTTER
FISH LIVER OIL

Meat, Fish, Eggs
CREAMED CHICKEN ON TOAST
LAMB CHOP
FISH
SCRAMBLED EGGS

CANADIAN CHEESE
Sandwich Fillings
COLD BEEF
PEANUT BUTTER
EGG SALAD

Desserts
CHOCOLATE PUDDING
ICE CREAM
CUSTARD
OATMEAL COOKIES

Bread and Cereal
TOAST
BRAN MUFFINS
OATMEAL
BREAD

What Do You Think?

1. In the cooking room at school, Jean noticed a poster with the title, "The most expensive diet is not always the best diet."

How would you explain what the title might mean?

2. Bill Porter didn't eat in the school lunchroom. Instead he ate at a food store across the street. One noon Sue saw him in there eating some doughnuts and drinking a bottle of pop!

"What an *awful* lunch, Bill!" she exclaimed. "Why don't you eat at school and get a good lunch?"

"Oh, run along," answered Bill. "I'm getting plenty to eat, and that's all that matters."

Do you agree with Bill that getting "plenty to eat" is all that matters? Why or why not?

3. Sam heard a radio announcer say: "*Everyone* needs vitamins. For your health's sake, buy a family-sized bottle of Starr's Vitamins today."

"Say, Mother," said Sam, "let's buy some."

Do you think Sam's family should buy the vitamins just because a radio announcer suggested it?

How might Sam's family get the vitamins they need without taking vitamin tablets?

If anyone in the family needs extra vitamins, who should be the one to tell him so?

"All My Plans Are Spoiled!"

"I'm sorry, Jane," said Mother as she came out of Grandmother's bedroom late Saturday morning, "but I don't think you should have your friends here after the magician's show this afternoon. Grandmother isn't well, and you'd disturb her."

"But Mother," exclaimed Jane, "you let me plan this afternoon's party over a week ago, and Harriet and Mae are counting on it. Oh, dear! There's no use making any plans around here. They're always spoiled!"

"But Jane," said her mother, "Grandmother——"

"Grandma spoils everything," grumbled Jane. "Things haven't been the same since she came here to live. She thinks I make too much noise. And she fusses when I don't do everything just right! Sometimes I wish she hadn't come here to stay."

"Jane, Jane," said her mother, "I understand how you feel, but you mustn't let your grandmother hear you say things like that. It would upset her very much. We asked her to come and live with us, and she has been a great help to all of us. I wouldn't be able to go to work during the week if she weren't here to look after you and Johnnie."

"But she *does* spoil things," Jane said.

"You feel that way today," answered her mother, "but you didn't feel like that when she took the trouble to make you an Indian costume for Paul Willis' party. And you were very glad to have her here two weeks ago, when you were in bed with a cold. She was the one who made your favorite custard, and she was the one who showed you so many interesting ways to amuse yourself."

"That's so," agreed Jane. "But Mother, I've been *counting* on this party so much. Do you really think it would bother Grandma if I went ahead and had it anyway?"

"Yes, I *do* think it would," her mother said. "I'm sorry, Jane, but things like this happen now and then in families. Our plans don't always work out just the way we'd like them to. And we have to learn to be thoughtful of others, even if it sometimes means changing or postponing our plans."

— "I don't know what Harriet and Mae will think," said Jane. "Yesterday I reminded them about the party and told them to save room for lots of ice cream. Now I have to tell them they can't come."

"Why, Jane," exclaimed her mother, "you just gave me an idea. I can't always arrange things this easily, but I see a way to help you today. Instead of buying some ice cream after the show and serving it to the girls here, you may take them to the Sweet Shop for ice cream. Maybe that will be almost as good as a party here at home."

"That's a *wonderful* idea!" cried Jane. "The girls will like that. I know they will. My plans aren't really spoiled at all. And I honestly wouldn't want to disturb Grandma. She's nice!"

WHEN THOUGHTFULNESS IS NEEDED

At first Jane wanted to go ahead and have her party at home even though her grandmother wasn't feeling well. What made her decide not to?

There will be many times when you, like Jane, will need to show a little thoughtfulness toward others in your family. It will help then to remember how much you appreciate similar thoughtfulness shown to you. *If you want to live happily in a family, you have to learn to "give and take." That is, you have to "give in" now and then to the needs and wishes of others. And you have to learn to "take" disappointments and occasional changes in plans without getting too upset.*

For example, there will be times when you must miss your favorite radio program because others in the family want to hear something else. There will be times when you will have to be as quiet as possible to avoid disturbing your father, who is resting—or some member of the family who is ill. Now and then you may have to set aside your own plans and help entertain a friend of the family who is visiting in your home.

Of course, it isn't always easy to have to change your plans or give up things you have been counting on. At such times you may be annoyed or cross.

But you won't stay that way long if you remember to follow some of the advice this book has given about ways of handling upset feelings and facing disappointments. What are some desirable ways of behaving at times like these? If you don't remember, read again pages 28 and 29 and page 111.

When have you recently had occasion to show thoughtfulness toward someone else in your family? What did you do? What else might you have done?

Which two pictures below show situations in which someone is being thoughtful of others? What is happening in the picture at the left?

What are some other situations you can describe in which showing thoughtfulness makes things pleasanter or more comfortable at home?

You've gone to my favorite kind of movie the past two Saturdays so this time we'll go to the "Western" you've been talking about. The movie guide says it's worth seeing.

Why should I stay in and entertain Bobby? What if he has been sick? He's getting better now, isn't he? Let him amuse himself. I want to go out and play with Carmela and Lucy.

If you are looking for something to do, Billy, why don't you and Jim help me make a bridge with my Erector Set?

There is another way of showing thoughtfulness, too. You can be careful not to go about saying things you know are likely to hurt another person's feelings.

You will remember that Jane was very upset about not being able to have her party at home. She helped get rid of some of her cross feelings by telling her mother all the ways "Grandma spoils things."

Jane's mother knew that there are times when everyone needs to "talk out" all the things that have been bothering him. So she listened to Jane sympathetically, and she didn't scold her for what she had said. But she did remind her that "you mustn't let your grandmother hear you say things like that. It would upset her very much."

You, too, will occasionally want to "talk out" your cross or unhappy feelings with someone, probably your mother or another older person who understands. But be careful not to go about saying to others things that are unkind, that aren't really very helpful, and that will only make them unhappy.

Take the matter of criticism. There are some things you may say once in a while that are helpful and are meant in a kindly way, although they are really criticism.

For example, you might tell your sister about a spot on her skirt so that she can remove it before she goes to school. But such statements as "I don't like those new shoes of yours; they make your feet look big" or "Why do you wear that hat? Red's not becoming to you" are unkind and not at all helpful. Such criticism makes others unhappy.

Instead of being critical in ways that are neither kind nor helpful, it is a good plan to try to give a compliment now and then. Watch for things you can honestly admire in members of your family and in your friends. There isn't anyone who doesn't like a compliment. And the other person's pleasure in your compliment makes *you* feel happier, too.

Look at the pictures of George as he talked to his family and a friend one morning. Would you like to have George in your family? Why not?

George sometimes complains that people don't seem to like him very well. What advice could you give him to help him get along better with others?

Why does our cooked cereal always have lumps in it? Over at Pete's house it's always smooth, and it tastes better, too.

I'm certainly glad I don't have to wear glasses like yours, Betty Jean. They make you look like an owl.

Hello, Shrimp! How did they happen to let a little fellow like you on the Boy Patrol?

SAFETY AT HOME

Jane's mother always feels safe when she leaves her two children at home with their grandmother. She feels that way because Grandmother is so very careful around the house.

Jane's grandmother knows that the largest number of accidents happen in the home. That's why she does all she can to try to prevent accidents there. "A safe place for everything, and everything in its place" is Grandmother's motto.

That motto is a good one for you to keep in mind, too. For it has been proved that most of the accidents in the home are caused by conditions that can be corrected. That means you can help at your house by checking to see that things are safe.

Look at the pairs of pictures below and on page 139. In which situations is an accident likely? How can each dangerous situation be corrected?

Now make a list of the rooms in your home. Under the name of each room write a list of safety checks that should be made in it from time to time. For example, under *Bathroom* you might write:

1. Are there containers for the soap?
2. Are the hot and cold taps labelled correctly?
3. Is there a rubber mat in the tub or are there handles to hold on to when getting in or out of the tub?
4. Are all bottles in the medicine cabinet properly labelled and all old medicines thrown away?

139

When Jane was complaining that "Grandma spoils everything," her mother reminded her that "you were very glad to have her here two weeks ago, when you were in bed with a cold."

What were some of the things Grandmother did for Jane when she was sick in bed? If you don't remember, read page 132 again.

Just as Jane did, you should go to bed when you have a cold. *The best treatment for a cold is plenty of sleep and rest in bed and lots of fruit drinks. It is also important that you keep away from others as much as possible. Why?*

Of course, when you have to stay in bed with a cold—or when you are in bed recovering from some other illness—the time seems to pass very slowly. That is when hobbies come in handy. And that is when you need to know many ways of amusing yourself.

In the pictures on page 141 you can see some of the ways Jane's grandmother helped her amuse herself when she was sick.

What does each picture show?

What are some of *your* favorite ways to amuse yourself when you are sick and have to stay in bed?

Suppose your younger brother is sick in bed with a cold and you can't go into the bedroom to amuse him. What toys and other materials might you send in to help him entertain himself?

Suppose your little sister is getting better from an illness and it is safe for you to go into her room to entertain her. What might you do to amuse her? What might you do for an older brother or sister?

"I'll Be the Only One"

"It looks like rain," said Elizabeth's mother. "Be sure to wear your rubbers, girls. And don't forget your raincoats. It may be pouring before you get to the magician's show at the high school."

"Do we have to?" asked Elizabeth. "It isn't raining yet, and maybe it won't. We don't want to be the only ones at the magician's show carrying all that stuff!"

At Jane's house her mother was saying, "Jane, I'm so sorry you left your raincoat in your locker at school. I'm afraid you're going to need it. Well, you'll just have to take Grandmother's big black umbrella. We can't have you getting soaking wet, especially on a cold day like this."

"Oh, Mother, not that gruesome thing!" cried Jane. "Why, it looks like a tent!"

"Never mind how it looks," said her mother. "It will keep you dry."

So Jane took the big black umbrella, but she didn't feel very happy about it.

"No one else will have an umbrella," she thought. "I'll be the only person who has to carry one. I wish I hadn't left my raincoat in my locker at school yesterday."

And at Allen's house his mother was calling, "Come back, Allen. Come and get your slicker. You'd better put on your high-top boots, too. I think there's going to be a heavy rain before you get back from the program."

"Mother," protested Allen, "I won't need my slicker or the high-top boots either. I hate to wear those things!"

"Just the same, take your slicker along," said his mother.

"Oh, all right," said Allen. So he got the high-top boots and the slicker and slowly started out.

"I'll look like a sissy loaded down with a slicker," he kept thinking. "I bet I'll be the only one in an outfit like this."

He stepped out the door of his apartment building and looked up and down Polk Street. Then a grin spread slowly over his face.

Going down the street was a parade of boys and girls, all heading toward the high school for the magician's show. There were Don, Sam, Jo Ann, Elizabeth, Thelma, Jane, Mae, and Harriet.

And as he looked at each one of them, Allen began to feel better and better. Can you see why?

Things for You to Think About

1. On the afternoon of the program at the high school the weather report on the radio forecast rain before night. But Allen, Jane, and the others didn't want to follow their parents' suggestions about taking along rain clothes.

What reasons did they give for not wanting to do what their mothers had suggested?

Of course, there are times when all boys and girls your age want to do what the others are doing. But there are other times when common sense is needed, regardless of what others may do.

What are some of the times when "using your head" is more desirable than insisting on doing what you think your friends will be doing?

2. "I know a quicker way to do dishes than Mother uses," said Lily. "I just hold the dishes under the hot-water tap. That gets them clean."

What suggestions could you give Lily about her way of doing dishes?

3. "My goodness!" said Ruth, who was reading a book about the Eskimos. "The Eskimos certainly eat lots more fatty foods than we do!"

How do you explain why the Eskimos might need more fatty foods than you do?

4. One Saturday, Philip invited some friends to his home to see a new cartoon strip on the family moving-picture machine. But after the boys came, Philip couldn't make the machine work, and his father wasn't home to help him. After fussing with the machine a while, Philip lost his temper. "This crazy old machine won't work," he shouted. "You fellows might as well go on home."

Of course Philip was disappointed that the machine wouldn't work, but do you think he met his disappointment in the best way? Why or why not?

What might he have done to "make the best of things" and to give his guests a more satisfying afternoon?

5. In this unit you have found the advice, "The fairest plan in a family is to have each one help according to his own age and ability."

What do you do to help at home?

Are you helping as best you can "according to your age and ability"? If not, what else might you do?

6. "I'd better squeeze this pimple," said Florence, "so that it will be gone before the party Friday."

Should Florence squeeze the pimple? Why not?

7. One day Paul walked through a patch of poison ivy with his high-top boots on. Later he found he had a poison-ivy rash on his hands.

How can you explain Paul's getting the rash on his hands when he hadn't handled the poison-ivy plants?

8. "Why do you wear that funny old blue coat?" Gertie said to Sarah one morning. "I wouldn't be seen in it."

"Oh, Gertie!" said Mabel, who was walking with the other two girls. "What a thing to say!"

"Well," said Gertie, "I always tell people what I think. And I think that coat is funny. So why shouldn't I say so?"

What do you think of Gertie's remark about Sarah's coat?

Do you think you should always tell other people "just what you think" about them or their clothes? Why do you think as you do?

9. One of Jim's brothers worked in an office, and the other one worked on a crane in a steel mill. Both brothers carried their lunches each day, but one carried much more food than the other one.

Which brother would need more food? Why do you think so?

10. One morning Emily noticed the picture you see above on the back sheet of the morning newspaper. "Look at this picture," she said to her brother Bob. "Every safety rule you can think of is shown in it."

Look at each safety rule in the picture. Why is each rule an important one to observe?

Do you think every safety rule is included in the picture or can you suggest others? If so, what are they?

Things for You to Do

1. Look at the picture of the "haunted house" that is shown below. Find at least five things happening in the house that might easily cause a fire.

Now draw another "haunted house." This time make up a set of situations showing carelessness that might cause other accidents in the home.

2. See if you can borrow from the school shop such tools as a hammer, saw, plane, awl, axe, and hatchet. Be ready to demonstrate correct and *safe* ways to use these tools.

3. In a First-Aid Handbook, or in the Boy Scout or the Girl Guide Handbook, look up the first-aid treatment for *cuts, burns, blisters,* and *sprained ankles.* Be ready to explain the treatments or make simple diagrams to show the treatments.

4. Make a chart showing all the kinds of foods you need to eat each day. Use the picture on page 127 to help you. Then put the chart in your kitchen at home where you and your mother can use it to check on your daily diet.

5. Make a scrapbook of good suggestions for "Things to Do" when you must stay in bed because of a minor illness.

6. Write about such topics as "My Biggest Worry," "My Worst Disappointment," "Why I Sometimes Quarrel with My Brothers and Sisters." These papers might be unsigned and used for class discussion about ways of solving some of the situations described.

7. Watch the newspaper for stories of accidents in the home. Be ready to tell how the accidents might have been avoided.

8. In what ways have you been able to change so that you get along better with your family?

9. In what ways have you been able to change so that you feel happier than you used to?

You

and School

"You're Growing Up"

"Why aren't you wearing your new school shoes, Elizabeth?" her mother asked. "We bought them several weeks ago and you haven't worn them at all."

"Well-ll," said Elizabeth, "I'll be wearing them soon, I guess, but——"

"If they aren't comfortable, we'll take them back and talk to the fitter at the shoe store," suggested her mother. "We took a great deal of care in buying your school shoes, but maybe they need to be stretched a little."

"Oh, no!" cried Elizabeth. "Not *stretched*, Mother. They're too big as it is. They make my feet look a mile long! That's why I hate to wear them.

"Here, I'll try them on again. You'll see what I mean!"

Then Elizabeth tried on the new shoes again.

"Well, now," said her mother as she looked at them, "they are a half size larger than your old ones, but I don't think they make your feet look much bigger. They are dark, and dark shoes always make feet look smaller. The cut-out pattern helps, too."

"Is that really true?" exclaimed Elizabeth. "Oh, I hope so! I worry all the time about my feet. It seems to me they get bigger every day. I even sit on them whenever I can, so people won't see how big they are. Won't they *ever* stop growing, Mother?"

"Why, Elizabeth, of course they will," said her mother. "Just remember that you're growing up. And different parts of you sometimes do their growing at different times. Just recently your feet have been growing. But sooner or later the other parts of your body will catch up with them."

"Sure," said her brother Ned. "I remember when everybody teased me about my big feet. But they don't look so big now."

"Of course they don't," said his mother, smiling. "The rest of you grew up to your feet, and now they aren't too big at all."

"My!" said Elizabeth with a sigh of relief. "You don't know how much better that makes me feel. My big feet just show that I'm growing up! I think I'll wear my new shoes to school today."

Much of Elizabeth's worry about her "big feet" could have been avoided if she had understood how boys and girls do their growing from the ages of ten to fourteen or sixteen.

And if you worry at times because you think your hands and feet are unusually large—or because you think you are too tall or not tall enough—the following information will help you, too.

You should know that physical growth goes on in spurts. Not all parts of your body grow at the same time, and not all parts reach their adult size at the same time. For example, your feet, hands, and brain may be fully grown a good while before your legs, arms, and trunk are.

During the years from ten to fourteen or sixteen, different parts of your body will be growing rapidly at different times. As a part reaches its adult size, its growth stops. Meanwhile other parts of your body continue their growing or begin growing. This goes on until all parts of your body are fully grown.

If you know how your body does its growing, you won't be too much concerned if your hands or feet, for example, seem for a time out of proportion to the rest of your body.

154

You needn't be concerned about being a little awkward, either. Some awkwardness is bound to result from the unevenness of growth of your bones and muscles and glands.

You should also keep in mind that *instead of making regular gains in height and weight, you are more likely to make sudden gains, or spurts.* For example, a gain of three to five inches in height and a gain of ten to fourteen pounds in weight in a year is not unusual for a girl about your age.

Before and after height and weight spurts there will be periods of time when little if any gains will be made. These periods in which little gains in height or weight are made are called *plateaus.*

Girls begin to grow taller and heavier at an earlier age than do boys. Most but not all girls make their biggest gains in height and weight sometime during the years between ten and thirteen. But a great many boys do not make their biggest spurts in height and weight until sometime between the ages of thirteen and sixteen.

That is why there are many girls in Grades Five to Eight who are taller than the boys in their class. But eventually the boys catch up, and in high school there are a great many boys who are as tall as or taller than the girls who are their classmates.

Each girl is eleven years old,
but each has a different body build.

You should remember that *every person is different and no two boys or no two girls the same age grow at exactly the same rate.*

Sooner or later all girls will make a spurt in height and weight, their bodies will round out, and changes will take place in their bodies to make them young women. But this happens to some girls several years before it happens to others of the same age.

Sooner or later all boys will make spurts in height and weight, their voices will become deeper, hair will grow on their faces, and changes will take place in their bodies to make them young men. But these changes take place in some boys at twelve, in others at thirteen, and in still others at fourteen, fifteen, or sixteen.

Since every person is different—with a different body build and a different rate of growing—you should not expect to make exactly the same gains in height or weight that your friends make.

You may sometimes wonder, "Is there something special I ought to do to make myself grow as I should?" Of course, if you are very, very fat or if you are very, very thin, you should see a doctor. But otherwise you really don't need to worry about growing if you keep healthy. Your body will take care of your growth at the rate that is right for you.

The important thing to keep in mind is this: EVERYTHING THAT HELPS MAKE YOU HEALTHY AND STRONG HELPS YOU GROW PROPERLY.

Each boy is the same age, but each has a different body build.

SHOES THAT FIT

You will remember that Elizabeth's mother said, "We took a great deal of care in buying your school shoes." This care had been taken because her mother knew how important it is that shoes fit well.

You should keep in mind, too, that well-fitting, comfortable shoes will help your feet grow straight and strong—and will keep you. from having foot troubles of one kind or another.

The picture on page 159 gives you some suggestions to follow when buying new shoes. What are they? Why is each suggestion a good one?

What suggestions are given in the picture on page 159 about stockings or socks? What advice is given about trimming the toenails?

The picture below shows some foot troubles caused by poorly fitting shoes. What are these difficulties? How can such foot troubles as these be prevented?

A painful swelling called a bunion is caused by too short or too narrow shoes that force the joints of the big toe out of line

Thickened places called corns are caused by too narrow or too pointed shoes that crowd the toes and rub the skin

Be sure the shoes are comfortable when you walk, as well as when you sit. Choose shoes with broad toes. Allow an extra three quarters of an inch in length.

To avoid crowding your toes, be sure your stockings are about half an inch longer than your feet.

To prevent ingrowing toenails, trim your toenails straight across.

YOUR POSTURE

Poorly fitting shoes not only cause foot troubles, but they also affect your posture. It is not easy to have good posture if your feet hurt with every step you take.

There is another thing that may affect your posture, and that is the sudden height gains children your age sometimes make. For example, some girls do not like the fact that they have suddenly become taller than most of their classmates, and they begin to slouch to hide their height.

Instead of realizing that such gains in height are quite normal—and instead of seeing that there are advantages in being tall and looking "grown up"— these girls try to hide their height by stooping over.

Which girl is doing this in the picture below? What advice would you give her?

There are other causes of poor posture, too. And as you learn what these causes are, you will see that having good posture is much more than a matter of just remembering to "sit up straight" or "stand up straight."

The way you feel has much to do with your posture. If you look around you, you will see that this is true. You can often tell by the way people walk, stand, or sit whether they are tired or unhappy. How does a person walk when he is discouraged? When he is pleased and happy?

Now look at the pictures of the children below. Which ones look unhappy? Which one looks tired? Which ones look happy and at ease?

If your posture is poor because you have unhappy feelings a great deal of the time, what might you do about the situation? You will find some good suggestions on pages 28 and 29 and page 111.

Strong muscles are also important to good posture. Your muscles help hold your bones in place and so help hold your body straight. And strong muscles do this work better than weak ones. To build strong  muscles you need a well-balanced diet and plenty of exercise.

Getting enough sleep is important, too. When you don't get the sleep you need night after night, it is hard for you to have good posture.

If you want good posture, be sure to wear shoes that fit. Be proud of your height and don't try to hide it. Keep cheerful. And above all, follow the rules for healthful living. These rules are shown below on posters made by boys and girls your age. What are the rules?

"All Mixed Up"

One Monday morning Allen came into the classroom with a new boy whom he introduced to Miss Thompson as Philip Rinaldo.

"Philip just moved here from Montreal," he said. "He lives in our block, and you ought to see him play ball! He's just what we need on our team."

Miss Thompson told Philip where to put his hat and coat, and she asked Allen to show him around the school to help him feel at home there.

When the boys came back, Miss Thompson was looking over Philip's record from his other school.

"You want a front seat, don't you?" she asked Philip.

"Oh, no, I really don't," protested Philip. "Let me sit in the back for a change."

"But you have trouble—" began Miss Thompson.

"Please," said Philip. "Let me try a back seat."

"Well-ll," said Miss Thompson, "you may try it for a while and see how it works out."

Just before recess the class had a spelling test. Miss Thompson pronounced the words, and the children wrote them on their papers. Time after time Philip asked to have the words repeated. Later, as the boys and girls checked their test papers, Philip sat looking quite discouraged.

"I got all mixed up on that test," he said, as he walked out to the playground with Miss Thompson.

"Maybe it was partly because your feelings are 'all mixed up,'" suggested Miss Thompson. "You know, Philip, you are a little hard of hearing, and you don't want to admit it, even to yourself. But sooner or later you'll *have* to admit it, because it's so. When you do admit it, you'll feel better. And you can do something about it, too."

"Like sitting in a front seat?" asked Philip.

"Yes," Miss Thompson replied, "and there are other ways we can work out together."

"Well-ll," said Philip, "I'll take that front seat. I guess I was sort of mixed up, but I begin to see——"

"Come on, Philip," called Allen. "The fellows want to see you throw that curve."

"Watch me," said Philip. "I'm not mixed up any more, but I can mix up those batters out there!"

DON'T TRY TO FOOL YOURSELF

Philip didn't like to admit that he was hard of hearing. So he tried to act as if he weren't. And that is the kind of mistake you may have made, too. It is a mistake we all sometimes make. We don't like to admit that there is anything wrong with us. So we try to fool ourselves about our weaknesses and act as if we didn't have them.

Miss Thompson gave Philip some good advice about his attempt to hide his hearing defect. What was her advice?

Like Philip, *you will find that you feel better when you admit your handicaps, whatever they may be.*

You will feel happier, too, if you always keep in mind that there isn't anyone in the world who is perfect. Every one of us can do some things well, but we all have difficulties or shortcomings of one sort or another.

Some people are born with certain physical handicaps, such as poor eyesight, poor hearing, lameness, or the like. Other people have speech defects. And still others have problems in making friends or in taking part in athletics or in artwork. Still others find it difficult to excel in such subjects as arithmetic, spelling, or history.

The first step in handling any difficulty you may have is to admit it. Then see if there is anything you can do about it. You will have to learn, too, to set goals that are reasonable and sensible for you in the light of any limitations you may have.

For example, if arithmetic is hard for you, you should do the best you can and ask for extra help when you need it. But you shouldn't get discouraged because you don't do so well as some of your friends who find arithmetic very easy.

If you have very poor eyesight, it often isn't wise to set your heart on being the *best* baseball or basketball player in your class. Enjoy these games, of course. But if you want to be a star, you may be more likely to succeed if you pick a sport like swimming or track where you won't need extra-good eyesight.

Now look at the children in the picture on page 167. Which ones are trying to fool themselves about their shortcomings? What advice could you give them?

Which ones are facing their shortcomings sensibly? What makes you think so?

What are some of *your* shortcomings? What have you just learned that may help you in feeling better and acting more sensibly about your own difficulties or handicaps?

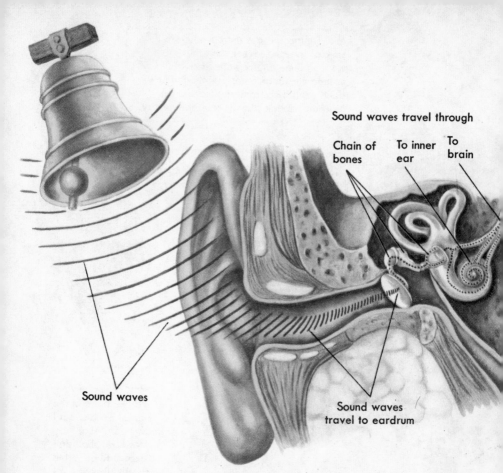

Sound waves travel through

Chain of bones

To inner ear

To brain

Sound waves

Sound waves travel to eardrum

YOUR EARS AND EYES

You know from Philip's experience and from your own experience that your ears and your sense of hearing are important in helping you do your schoolwork. So are your eyes and your sense of seeing. But your sense of seeing and your sense of hearing not only help you with schoolwork. They help keep you safe, and they help you enjoy life. How?

Your senses of seeing and of hearing are probably the most important of all your five senses. And that is why you should know about the different parts of your eyes and ears and how they work. It is also very important that you know how to take care of your eyes and your ears.

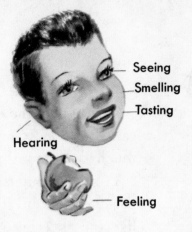

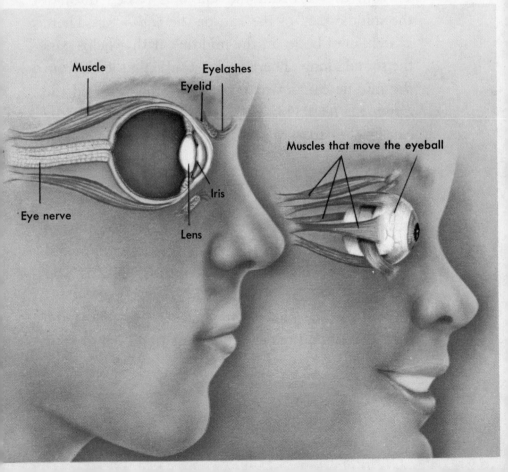

The part of the ear that you can see is sometimes called the *outer ear*. This part helps catch sounds much as the mouthpiece of a telephone does.

From the outer ear the sound goes along a little passageway until it reaches a skinlike part that looks like the covering on a drum. This skinlike part is called the *eardrum*.

From the eardrum the sound is passed through the middle part of the ear, or the *middle ear*. There is a chain of bones in the middle ear that helps pass the sound along. There is also a tube that leads from the middle ear down to the throat. It is called the *Eustachian tube*. This tube brings air into the middle ear, for the eardrum needs air on both sides of it to do its work well.

From the middle ear the sound is passed to the *inner ear*, which is filled with a liquid. The sound waves make this liquid begin moving, and the moving causes the nerves in the inner ear to send sound messages to your brain. When this happens, you *hear*.

Now use the picture on page 168 to follow the path that sound makes from your outer ear to your inner ear.

HOW YOU SEE

Your eyeball is a firm but rather soft ball filled with a clear, watery liquid. Over the front of your eyeball there is a colorless cover, called the *cornea*. And in the colored part, or *iris,* of the eyeball is a little opening called the *pupil*.

Just behind the cornea and the pupil is the *lens*. And at the back of the eyeball is the lining, or *retina,* part of which is made of nerve tissue.

Your eye works much like a camera. For example, when you look at a dog, the likeness, or *image,* of the dog is carried by rays, or beams, of light through the cornea and pupil of each eye, to the lens, and then to the retina.

When the image of the dog gets to the retina, a wonderful thing happens. The retina, which is like the film inside the camera, takes a picture of the dog. This picture, like all pictures on the retina, is upside down. Then the nerves of the retina send a message about the picture to the brain. Your brain makes it clear to you what the picture is, and you *see* a dog.

Now use the picture on page 169 to follow the path of light rays through the eye to the brain.

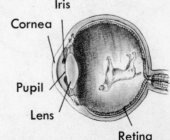

Iris
Cornea
Pupil
Lens
Retina

171

TAKING CARE OF YOUR EARS

Have you ever been in a movie when something went wrong with the sound effects? If so, you know how odd it seems to see lips moving and actions taking place on the screen but to hear no conversation or other sounds. That gives you a little idea of what it would be like if you were without your sense of hearing.

Because your sense of hearing is so important in keeping you in touch with what is going on around you, and in helping you enjoy life, you want to be sure to take good care of your ears.

Most of the suggestions about the care of the ears centre on four situations: *when you are washing your ears; when you are playing; when you have a cold or some disease such as scarlet fever; and when you have an earache.*

The picture below and the ones on the next page give some suggestions about each of these situations. What are they? What suggestions can you add?

Never use anything smaller than a finger inside a washcloth to clean out your ears.

If you use sharply pointed objects such as hairpins or match sticks, you may pierce your eardrum.

When you swim or dive, it's a good plan to wear a bathing cap or put plugs in your ears. Water that gets into the ear usually drains out quickly. But in the case of a damaged eardrum, the water may enter the middle ear and cause serious trouble.

When you have a cold, be sure to blow your nose gently. If you blow too hard, you may force mucus up the Eustachian tube and into the middle ear. This may cause an infection in the ear.

The ears should be watched carefully by a doctor during and after such diseases as scarlet fever, measles, and diphtheria.

TISSUES

JOHN B. WALKER, M.D.
EAR - NOSE
AND THROAT

An earache is a sign of trouble in the middle ear. If you have an earache, you should see a doctor. He can do something to stop the ache, and he can help prevent any damage to your hearing.

TAKING CARE OF YOUR EYES

One of the first things you think of in considering how to take care of your eyes is the need for proper light when you read or study. Getting enough light of the right kind is most important in helping protect your eyesight.

You know, of course, how to get the best light when you are reading. If you are right-handed, you try to sit so that the light from a window or from a lamp comes over your left shoulder and onto your book. This helps avoid shadows on your book and helps keep light from being reflected back into your eyes.

What should you do about reading light if you are left-handed?

Perhaps you are not so sure about how to get proper light when you are working at a desk or table. Two things that you should try to avoid are shadows and glare. The pictures below and at the top of page 175 give you suggestions about avoiding harmful shadows and glare. What are the suggestions?

An unshaded or improperly shaded light bulb produces a direct glare. This can be avoided by using shades of the proper type that completely cover the bulb.

Shadows are much more tiring to the eyes than you may realize. Be sure when you are writing or reading or doing close work that the light comes from the side opposite the hand being used.

It is very tiring to your eyes to work in a "pool" of light surrounded by dark shadows. Even though you are working with a lamp close at hand, have some other light in the room, too.

Another thing to remember is that a steady light for reading is better than an unsteady or flickering light. Reading in cars, buses, or trains may cause eyestrain because the unsteady light and the movement of the car make the eyes do extra work to keep the words in focus.

Sitting too close to the screen at the movies may also strain your eyes. That's why it is a good plan to sit about halfway back or farther in the theatre.

When you read, write, sew, or do other close work, your eyes tire more quickly than usual. At times like these you should look away from your book or your work now and then. By looking away you give your eye muscles a chance to rest.

If your eyes burn after you have been reading or doing close work, if letters on a page are blurred, if your eyelids twitch, or if you have many headaches, you should see an eye doctor and have your eyes examined. He may find that you have an eye defect that can be corrected if you wear glasses. Or he may find that you have been straining your eyes by reading with poor light.

Of course, you must not only be sure to give your eyes proper light. You must also help protect them from accidents and injuries. For example, you should be very careful with sharp and pointed objects such as sticks, arrows, scissors, and knives. What precautions should you take?

Careless throwing of dirt, stones, or hard snowballs may also cause eye injuries. What are some suggestions that will help avoid such injuries?

Air rifles, other guns, and fireworks have also caused many injuries to the eyes. What safety rules can help prevent such accidents?

One more thing to remember is to use your own towel and washcloth at home and to use clean towels in washrooms away from home. By doing this, you can avoid getting an eye disease, such as pinkeye, which is passed from one person to another by the use of common washcloths and towels.

YOUR HEALTH AND SAFETY AT SCHOOL

Because you use your eyes a great deal at school, special efforts are made to have enough light of the right kind in each classroom.

Look around your classroom. What evidences do you see that attention has been given to proper lighting? Are there any improvements in lighting that you think could be made?

The school does other things, too, to protect your health and to keep you safe from accidents. The pictures below and on the next page show some of the things Allen's school does to help promote good health. What does each picture show? Why is each of these things important?

Now be ready to tell how *your* school helps promote good health. Also be ready to suggest any improvements you think might be made.

The pictures below show some of the things Allen's school does to help keep the pupils safe from accidents. What does each picture show?

What does *your* school do about safety?

What can *you yourself* do to help avoid accidents in school, on the school playgrounds, and on the way to school?

What Do You Think?

1. Sally Martin was quite upset one day when she and her classmates were being weighed and measured. "I'm the tallest one in the class," she thought. "It looks as if I'm always going to be taller than everyone else, even the boys!"

What could you tell Sally to cheer her up?

2. When Helen was reading some advertisements for girls' clothes, she saw this sign under a picture: CLOTHES THAT HELP YOU THROUGH THE AWKWARD AGE. "Now why should any age be called 'the awkward age'? " thought Helen.

Can you explain why the years from ten to sixteen are sometimes called "the awkward age"?

3. Bob needed a new pair of shoes, but he couldn't seem to find time to go downtown with his mother to buy them. "Why don't you just go down and buy me a pair?" Bob asked his mother. "You know my size."

What reasons can you give why Bob's mother should not buy the shoes unless he is along?

4. "It's easy to have good posture," Paul explained to his cousin Tom. "All you have to do is to practise walking around the house with a book on your head. When you can walk without the

book falling off, you'll know you have good posture."

Does Paul's advice include all that is necessary for good posture? What would you add?

5. Jean had been having some headaches, and her mother had decided to take her to an eye doctor. But Jean didn't want to go. "If I have eye trouble, I don't want to know it," she said. "I might have to wear glasses and that would be *terrible!*"

What do you think about Jean's attitude? What advice would you give her?

6. Jack got up one morning with a bad cold, and he complained that he could hardly breathe. "Blow your nose hard," suggested his sister Nell. "Then you'll feel better."

Did Nell give Jack good advice? Why not?

7. "Let's hurry," said Peg one Saturday as she and Sarah started to a movie. "If we get there early enough, we can get seats right up in the front row."

What do you think of Peg's choice of seats?

8. "There's a lot of wax in your ear, Mary," said Sue. "Here's a bobby pin to get it out."

"Oh, no," said Mary. "I know a safer way."

What do you think the safer way was? Why was the way Sue suggested not safe?

"One of Those Things"

In the quiet classroom Kenneth sat playing with the pages of the book he was supposed to be reading. He looked at the faces of the other boys and girls and thought a little resentfully, "*They* can enjoy reading. They don't have to do what I have to after school!" He could feel his heart thumping hard as he thought about it, and his hands were damp with perspiration. Now and then he touched his left jaw and frowned.

Once Miss Thompson saw him frown, and she noticed that he wasn't enjoying his library book. She walked over to him and asked in a low voice, "Ken, don't you feel well, or is something worrying you?"

Ken answered, "You know, Miss Thompson, all I can think about is going to the dentist this afternoon. I wish I didn't have to go!"

"So that's why you aren't reading!" exclaimed Miss Thompson. "What is it, just a check-up?"

"No, he's going to fill a back tooth that's been hurting lately," Ken said.

"Well, I suppose nobody really *wants* to have a tooth filled," answered Miss Thompson. "But it's one of those things we have to face. It may help you if you think about it this way: What would happen if you neglected the tooth?"

Ken looked a little puzzled. Then he said, "I guess it would get worse."

"Exactly," said Miss Thompson, "and it would become more and more painful. Eventually you might lose the tooth, and you know how important it is to keep all your teeth. So it's better to get the job done before the tooth gets too bad. A little pain now is better than a lot of pain later."

Ken felt a little better, after having a chance to talk over his trouble with someone who listened and understood.

On the way to the dentist's after school he kept thinking over and over, "A little pain now is better than a lot of pain later." And he even began to whistle as he walked along!

Often you, like Kenneth, will have some trouble or problem that makes you feel unhappy or dissatisfied. You, too, may be upset about having to go to the dentist. You may worry about having to wear glasses or needing braces on your teeth. You may be unable to plan to go to Scout Camp with your friends next summer because your family can't afford it.

There are several ways you might meet problems like these. You might act as Kenneth did at first—make yourself miserable by thinking again and again about the unpleasant situation and by feeling very sorry for yourself. Or you might do a lot of wishful thinking about ways to get out of doing what you know really must be done. But these are not very helpful ways of handling unpleasant situations, and they are ways that don't make you feel any better.

A better way to face something that is making you unhappy is to stop and think, "Is there anything that can be done about this?" If there is, set about doing it. For example, you might find a way to earn the money needed to take you to Scout Camp with your friends.

Often, however, there isn't anything to be done about a situation except to "take it" and make the best of it. We all have to learn to put up with some things that aren't exactly as we would like to have them.

It usually helps at times like these to talk to someone who understands and who may be able to help, as Miss Thompson helped Kenneth.

It also helps if you will try to find something good in the situation and think about that instead of continually fussing about the unpleasant side. For example, instead of complaining about wearing glasses, you might think, "Oh, well, these glasses are helping me do better work at school, and they are keeping me from having headaches."

Which picture below shows the more helpful way of facing a problem? What makes you think so?

What unpleasant situation have *you* had to face recently? Did you make the best of it?

I'll cry and make a big fuss, and maybe Dad will say I don't have to wear the braces on my teeth after all.

I guess I'm not the only one who has to wear braces. And anyway by the time I get to high school, I'll have nice straight teeth.

Clean, healthy teeth add much to your
attractiveness and save you
pain from aching or infected teeth.

Aching teeth take the joy out of life
and make it hard for you to work or
play as usual.

ALL ABOUT YOUR TEETH

You read about Kenneth and how his worry
over the trip to the dentist kept him from enjoying his library book at school one day. But you
didn't read how his toothache the day before made
him miserable and kept him from playing ball.

However, you may know from your own experience that aching teeth make it hard for you to study
and hard for you to work or play as usual. That's
one reason why it is important to know about your
teeth and to know how to give them good care.

And of course you want to know how strong,
healthy teeth are built. For a complete set of healthy
teeth helps you chew your food properly, helps
make you more attractive, and helps you pronounce
correctly words with such letters as *f, g, j,* and *s*
in them.

HOW YOUR TEETH GROW

When you were born, all your first teeth, or *primary teeth*, were partly formed and were in your jawbone. The tooth cells from which your second teeth, or *permanent teeth,* form were also in your jawbone.

Each of your teeth grows in a little *sac,* or bag, in the jawbone. There are twenty sacs for your first set of teeth and thirty-two sacs for your permanent teeth.

These sacs are filled with a jellylike material made up of enamel-making cells, dentine-making cells, nerves, and blood vessels. The cells take from the blood the materials needed for building teeth. Most important among these materials are the minerals calcium and phosphorus.

After the *enamel* is formed, the enamel-making cells disappear. That is why your teeth, once they are formed, can never make any new enamel.

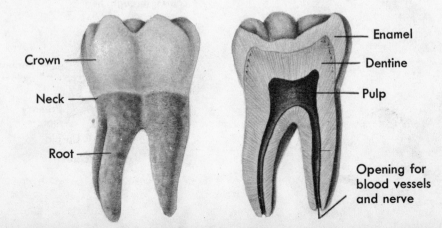

Crown

Neck

Root

Enamel

Dentine

Pulp

Opening for
blood vessels
and nerve

After the *dentine,* or bonelike material under the enamel, is formed, a few dentine-making cells remain. These cells can build more dentine in a tooth as long as the tooth is alive and healthy.

As each tooth grows larger, the sac in which it started shrinks and becomes the *pulp* in the centre of the tooth. A network of blood vessels and nerves is formed in the pulp. These nerves and blood vessels leave the tooth through a little tunnel, or *root canal,* which goes down each root.

The first teeth to come through the jaw are the front teeth, or *incisors.* Next come the *first* primary *molars,* then the *cuspids,* and finally the *second* primary *molars.* By the time you are two and a half or three years old, all twenty of your first set of teeth are in place.

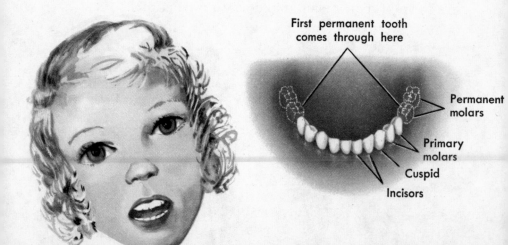

First permanent tooth comes through here

Permanent molars

Primary molars

Cuspid

Incisors

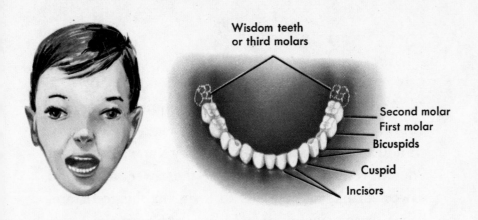

Wisdom teeth
or third molars

Second molar
First molar
Bicuspids
Cuspid
Incisors

When you were about six years old, the first of your permanent teeth appeared. These are the *six-year* molars. You can see them above and in the picture on page 188. These are very important teeth because they do the heavy work of chewing while the baby molars are falling out and the permanent *bicuspids* are coming in.

By the time you are twelve or thirteen, all of your first teeth have come out and twenty-eight of the permanent set have appeared. The last four of your permanent teeth, often called the *wisdom teeth,* come in when you are seventeen to twenty-one.

The picture above shows a twelve-year-old's mouth with twenty-eight permanent teeth in it. Have you this many teeth? Which teeth have yet to grow in your mouth? About when will they come in?

WHAT CAUSES TEETH TO DECAY?

As you know, your teeth feel quite strong and hard. But even so they can be broken down by *decay*. The cause of decay is not actually known, but most dental-research workers think that sweet foods and sweet drinks cause acids to form on the teeth and that these acids make holes, or *cavities*, in the teeth.

Decay always begins from the outside of the tooth and not from the inside. It usually begins in pits of the teeth, in cracks in the enamel, or between the teeth where bits of food have lodged. Decay, once it has broken through the enamel, spreads rapidly because the layer of dentine is softer than the enamel.

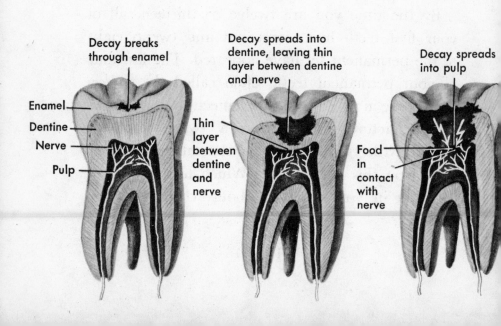

Decay breaks through enamel

Decay spreads into dentine, leaving thin layer between dentine and nerve

Decay spreads into pulp

Enamel
Dentine
Nerve
Pulp

Thin layer between dentine and nerve

Food in contact with nerve

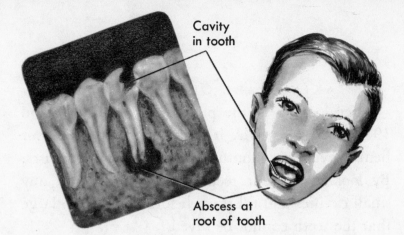

Cavity
in tooth

Abscess at
root of tooth

If a tooth is neglected after the decay has spread into the dentine, the decay will usually attack the pulp of the tooth. As the decay comes near the pulp, a very painful toothache will occur. And as the decay injures the pulp, it becomes much more difficult for a dentist to save the tooth.

Germs, or *bacteria,* may also enter the tooth and travel down through the pulp to the roots. Here the bacteria may cause pus, or an *abscess,* to form. Sometimes the bacteria, or the poisons which they give off as they grow, may get into the blood stream and help to cause serious trouble, such as heart disease or rheumatism.

If an abscess forms, help from a dentist is needed at once. The dentist can find out if there is an abscess at the root of a tooth by using his X ray. The X ray also helps him discover even the hidden decayed places between the teeth.

After looking at the pictures on pages 190 and 191, you can see why it is important to visit your dentist every six months or as often as he advises. By looking at your teeth often, he can find any small cavities and fill them before they get so large that the teeth cannot be saved.

You can also see why it is important to brush your teeth regularly and thoroughly. By doing this, you help remove the bits of sweet and starchy foods that form acids on the teeth and help cause cavities.

Teeth and gums should be brushed after each meal if possible. At the very least, they should be brushed twice a day—after breakfast and again at bedtime. If you can't brush your teeth, rinse your mouth well with water.

You have learned that your teeth grow for some years beneath the gums before they come through the gums. During these teeth-forming years, you should have a well-balanced diet which includes foods that are rich in the teeth-building minerals, calcium and phosphorus.

And even after your teeth are through the gums, a well-balanced diet helps keep the bones and gums around the teeth healthy.

Perhaps one of the most important things of all for you to keep in mind is that candy and other sweets are harmful to the teeth.

Most dental-research workers believe that people would have far less tooth decay if they would avoid eating too many sweet foods.

One way to avoid the damage that too many sweet foods can cause to your teeth is to eat fresh fruit for desserts more often than you eat such sweets as pies and cakes. Eating fruit, such as oranges, apples, or bananas, between meals is a good habit to form instead of eating candy or other sweets for between-meal snacks.

Now look at the posters below. Each one suggests something that will aid in taking care of the teeth. But each poster needs a paragraph to explain it. What explanation can you give for each one?

"I Failed the Test!"

"We're having a review test in arithmetic today," Elizabeth whispered to Jane, who had just come back after doing an errand for Miss Thompson. "It's the test on page 189 in our books."

"Oh, dear!" thought Jane. "I didn't do so very well the last time we had a test. I'll have to work harder on this one."

When Jane looked at the test, she felt encouraged. It was on dividing whole numbers, and she was better at that than with fractions.

Some of the boys and girls were through in a very short time, but Jane didn't take any chances. She worked very slowly, and she went over her paper carefully in the few minutes she had before Miss Thompson said, "It's time to stop now."

Then Miss Thompson asked for volunteers to put each problem on the blackboard, and the others checked their examples with those on the board.

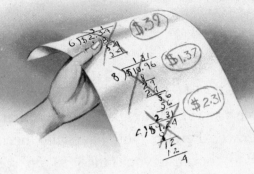

But it took only one or two examples to show Jane what she had done. She had forgotten to put in the dollar sign and the cents' point in each of her examples. That made every problem wrong!

After class she stopped to talk to Miss Thompson, and almost in tears she explained, "Wait till you see my paper. I forgot the dollar signs and cents' points, and so I failed the test. It's just *terrible* to fail like that, isn't it?"

"Why no, Jane," said Miss Thompson, "it's no disgrace to fail if you have honestly done your best. And you did do that today, didn't you?"

"Yes," said Jane. "But I still got zero."

"Well, of course, you don't want to go on doing that," Miss Thompson continued, "but you can learn from your failures, you know. I'm sure you've learned something worth while today."

"Oh, I have," cried Jane. "I've learned to be careful in problems with money. I bet I'll never again forget to put dollar signs and cents' points where they belong!"

Have you, like Jane, had the idea that a failure is a disgrace? Perhaps you have also been miserable at school because you failed to do something as well as others did.

If so, remember that *a failure is no disgrace if you have honestly tried hard and have done your very best at a task.*

You should also remember that *most failures can be made worth while.* For example, Jane's failure to place the dollar signs and cents' points correctly will probably result in her not making the same mistake again.

Elizabeth made a mistake in cooking class one day. She didn't notice that the recipe for salad dressing said to add the salad oil a few drops at a time. She added it all at once and later discovered her salad dressing wasn't properly thick and creamy. What do you think Elizabeth learned from her mistake?

Keeping in mind that you can learn something from failures will help keep you happier in your work at school. Most people experience failure now and then. Not all of them profit from their failures. Do you? What situation can you think of in which you learned something from a failure?

The cartoons on this page and on the next two pages give you some other suggestions on how to keep happy at school. What does each picture show? What suggestions can *you* add about ways of getting along happily at school?

The knowledge that you look right for school and that you are clean, neat, and appropriately dressed is satisfying.

NOT THIS

BUT

THIS

NOT THIS

BUT

THIS

You feel more comfortable when you keep to the required rules at school, such as being on time, observing traffic rules in the hall, and avoiding disturbing others during study periods.

Make an effort to contribute to class interest and activities. When you aren't contributing, you are likely to feel irritable or dissatisfied with yourself.

Trying to get out of doing something you should do fools no one but yourself. You are the one who loses, not the teacher.

I've just got to beat Don and Bill on this spelling test. I'm sick of being one of the worst spellers in the room.

NOT THIS

BUT

THIS →

Well, I've studied hard, and I'm going to do the best I can on this test. I ought to do better than I did last time.

You will feel happier and more comfortable if you learn to "do the best for you" instead of trying to compete with others in your class.

What? Did you get only 5 of the problems right? Look at my paper. I got them all right!

I may get along better in arithmetic than you, Sue, but don't forget how much better you are in reading than I am.

NOT THIS

BUT

THIS →

Bragging about your success is not being a good sport, especially if it makes someone else unhappy.

Things for You to Think About

1. Bert's mother had been having a form of rheumatism called *arthritis*. The doctor told her it might be caused partly by the infected teeth in her mouth. "That's funny," thought Bert. "How can infected teeth cause a disease like that?"

Can you explain how bad teeth may cause trouble in another part of the body?

2. The story is often told that Eskimo people, although they did not clean their teeth or go to the dentist, had very strong teeth and little decay until visitors came to their land. With the visitors came ideas about new kinds of foods, made of white flour and sugar. Before long the Eskimos, too, began to have "tooth troubles."

Do you think the new kinds of food the Eskimos learned to eat caused decay in their teeth? Why?

3. Bill Porter was angry when he learned that the sale of fireworks was forbidden by law in his town. "That's a fine thing," grumbled Bill. "We can't have any fun in this town any more."

Bill forgot that there was a good reason for forbidding the sale of fireworks. What was it?

4. "Why bother to see a dentist about your toothache?" said Jane to her cousin Betty.

"Why don't you buy some medicine at the drug store to kill the pain? That's quicker and easier."

Did Jane give her cousin good advice? What makes you think as you do?

5. Sam's family was going to move to a new town, and Sam was very unhappy about it. "I'll never forgive Dad for taking that new job," he kept thinking. "I just know I won't like the new school I'll have to go to, and I'll probably never find any good friends like Bill and Pete. I'll never have so much fun any more!"

Was Sam trying to make the best of a difficult situation? How might he have helped himself feel better about it?

6. There was always a bowl of fruit around at Tim's house, and most of the family had the habit of eating an apple between meals or before going to bed.

What are some of the advantages in this habit?

7. "You won't catch me eating at the school cafeteria," said Thelma. "I'd rather eat at the corner store. Nobody there cares what you eat, and you can get pop, cookies, and a candy bar for a quarter."

What do you think of Thelma's plan for eating her lunch? What are your suggestions for a good noon meal when you carry a lunch? When you buy your lunch?

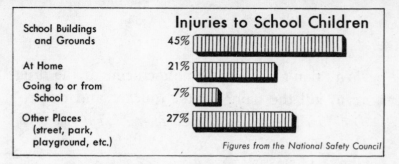

Injuries to School Children

School Buildings and Grounds	45%
At Home	21%
Going to or from School	7%
Other Places (street, park, playground, etc.)	27%

Figures from the National Safety Council

Things for You to Do

1. Study the graph above to learn *where* most of the accidents to school children occur, as found in one study made of such accidents. Then be ready to tell or to write a list of *how* such accidents might have happened.

2. Make up a School Safety Code to use as a means of helping avoid accidents in your school.

3. Keep a list for one month of all the accidents that occur at school to children in your class. Then plan how such accidents can be avoided in the future.

4. Make a safety calendar, with a safety picture for each month of the year.

5. Write suggestions for a "What Should You Do?" quiz program. Use ideas you learned in this unit. For example:

    a. If you want to have good light when studying at your desk, what should you do?

    b. If you have an earache, what should you do about it?

You and Your Community

SEWAGE-TREATMENT WORKS

"The Whole Story"

There was going to be a Health Exhibit in Allen's school, and all the people in Williston were to be invited to see it.

Allen's class had been asked to prepare a display of posters about keeping healthy.

"Let's pick out the best ones we've made this year," Miss Thompson suggested.

Later Kenneth was looking at the posters that had been chosen. "Say!" he exclaimed. "If everyone in Williston follows all our suggestions, they'll stay healthy all right."

Everyone in the class agreed with Kenneth. Everyone but Jane.

KEEPING HEALTHY
What YOU should do

"Our posters don't tell the whole story," Jane insisted. "Everyone in Williston could follow all these suggestions and still not stay healthy."

"Why, Jane," exclaimed Elizabeth, "can't you see that our posters tell about all the important ways of keeping healthy—ways like getting good food, plenty of sleep, lots of fresh air and exercise? We even have a poster about avoiding the spread of germs and one about happy feelings."

"All the same," said Jane, "we have told only what *we* should do. We haven't told what others must do for us."

"What do you mean?" asked Allen. "We have to keep *ourselves* healthy. Others can't help us."

"Oh, yes, they can!" answered Jane. "Just suppose our drinking water weren't kept safe for us. Or suppose people with diseases like scarlet fever weren't kept away from us. We could follow all the suggestions on our health posters, but a lot of us would probably get sick."

"Jane is right," Miss Thompson said. "Our posters tell just part of the story of how we keep healthy. There are some things we must do, but there are other things our community must do."

"Well, then," said Kenneth, "we'll have to make some more posters."

"But first we'll have to do some studying," Elizabeth added. "We'll have to find out all the things our community does to keep us healthy."

After learning how their community helped
people keep healthy, the class made a second
set of posters and placed them beside the first set.

Then even Jane agreed that if all the suggestions on all the posters were followed, Williston
people would be very healthy indeed!

THE WORK OF
THE HEALTH DEPARTMENT

Perhaps you have thought that your health depends only upon taking good care of yourself and upon following the rules for healthful living. But on second thought you can see that living in a healthful community is of equal importance.

If your drinking water were not kept safe, for example, you and others in your community might get typhoid fever or some other disease.

It is also important that the milk you drink be kept pure. Unpasteurized milk can cause such diseases as typhoid fever, sore throat, and tuberculosis.

If the foods you buy in stores and restaurants were not protected by inspection and by certain laws about cleanliness, food poisoning might occur and disease germs might be spread.

The posters on page 207 suggest a few of the many ways in which a community can help protect the health of its people. What are these ways?

Before Jane's class could make these posters, they had to do a lot of studying and investigating. First of all, they tried to find the answer to the question, "Who is responsible for keeping the community as healthful as possible?"

Philip suggested that there was probably a health department in Williston. He said he knew there was one in the city where he used to live.

So the class sent a committee to the Town Hall to ask about the health department and its work. The committee learned that their town, Williston, which was a fairly small town in Pine County, did not have a health department of its own. Instead the people were served by a Board of Health with head-quarters a few miles away.

"Each province in Canada has health districts or local health units," a man at the Town Hall told the committee. "A health unit is made up of a county or group of townships, together with cities, towns, and villages, which work together to take care of the health needs of all the people in the communities that make up the unit. Our town's health needs are well taken care of by our Health Unit under the direction of our Board of Health. But our Board could not do nearly so much for us if it were not for all the help it receives from the provincial Department of Health."

Then the man told the committee that they should write to the provincial Department of Health for information about the way the health needs of the people of Williston were cared for.

From the material they received, Jane's class learned that *two of the main duties of any health department, whether it is a local or provincial department, are to improve sanitary and health conditions and to help check the spread of disease.*

In carrying out these duties health departments usually do these things:

1. Keep records of all the births, marriages, and deaths.

2. Enforce regulations to check the spread of communicable diseases. Acquaint the public with isolation and quarantine regulations, and recommend inoculation against such diseases as smallpox, lockjaw, whooping cough, and diphtheria. They also provide these inoculations without charge for those who are unable to pay for them.

3. Inspect dairies, restaurants, ice-cream factories, and food stores to see if they are clean. If the standards of cleanliness are not met, health departments have authority to see that something is done about it.

4. Test samples of drinking water to be sure the water is safe for people to use.

5. By agreement with school boards, make health examinations. In some communities the entire responsibility for these things is taken by the school board rather than by the health department.

6. Set up clinics where mothers can bring babies for weighing and measuring and for health examinations.

7. Try to get rid of flies, mosquitoes, rats, and other pests, and check to see that garbage and rubbish are safely disposed of and that sewage is properly taken care of.

8. Give out information about healthful living through booklets, posters, talks, newspapers, and radio programs.

Jane's class learned that health departments employ many workers to carry out these important duties. The charts on pages 212, 213, and 214 show who some of these workers are and some of their duties. They will help you to understand some of the services that are usually provided by health departments.

If the workers in a local health department need help in carrying out their duties, to whom can they turn?

YOUR LOCAL HEALTH DEPARTMENT

All the provinces of Canada have well organized health services. If you live in an organized municipality, your community will be served by a local health department, even if it has not a health department of its own. This local health department may have from ten or twelve to many hundreds of workers in it, depending upon the number of people in the area it serves.

But whether your local health department is large or small, the main duties are much the same. And back of your local health department are the provincial Department of Health and the Department of National Health and Welfare, which are always ready to help communities to solve their health problems.

The chart below and on pages 213 and 214 shows how the Pine County Health Unit was organized.

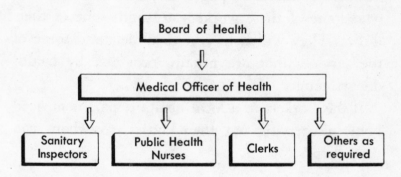

PINE COUNTY HEALTH UNIT

This doctor is the Director or Medical Officer of Health. He directs all the work of the Health Unit.

THE
SANITARY
INSPECTOR

The sanitary inspector covers the area for which he is responsible.

His work includes:

Inspecting restaurants and dairies in his area to be sure they are clean

Gathering samples of drinking water for testing in a laboratory to be sure it is safe for people to use

Gathering samples of milk to be sure it is safe

Checking to be sure that sewage and garbage are properly taken care of in the area

NURSES

Some duties of the public health nurses are:

Promoting health work in the schools

Making home visits

Helping at well-baby clinics

Helping with the program of public immunization

CLERKS

The clerks keep records, take telephone messages, receive visitors who come to the office, take care of the mail, and do other office work.

PROVINCIAL DEPARTMENT OF HEALTH

The local health department can at any time call for help from the provincial Department of Health.

The laboratory for examining water, sewage, and diagnostic specimens is usually at the provincial department headquarters, with branches in larger local communities.

Every doctor must report at once to the health department any case of contagious disease. And so must any other person who knows of such a case.

PREVENTING COMMUNICABLE DISEASES

While they were studying the work of local health departments, Allen's class learned how they help check the spread of communicable diseases.

They learned that every doctor must report at once to the health department any case of a communicable disease, and so must every other citizen who knows of such a case. Then the health department sees that a warning sign is placed on the house or apartment in cases where quarantine is required.

Whenever possible, a public health nurse from the health department visits the family of the person who has a communicable disease. She explains the reason and the need for following the doctor's orders, and when necessary, she demonstrates the care to be given the patient.

215

To protect other members of the family from the disease, the patient is kept in *isolation*, or kept in a room away from everyone but the doctor and the person who is caring for him.

The doctor and the family member caring for the patient take special care not to carry germs from the sickroom and spread them to others. They wash their hands thoroughly before and after taking care of the patient. The dishes that the patient uses are kept separate from other dishes and are boiled after each meal.

Besides making sure that persons with communicable diseases are isolated, the health department keeps a careful watch over those who have been exposed to the disease.

For example, if one child in a neighborhood becomes ill with scarlet fever, the children who have had close enough contact with him to breathe in germs of the disease—or who have used his books or toys—are exposed to the disease.

The way the health department watches children who have been exposed to a disease is to keep them out of school until the *incubation period* of the germs is over. Grown-ups are not usually isolated except for serious diseases such as smallpox, meningitis, or diphtheria.

By incubation period is meant the period of time between the entrance of the germs into the body and the time when the germs have multiplied enough to cause the first real symptoms of the disease.

For example, school children who have been exposed to whooping cough and who have not had this disease are often kept out of school for twelve days after their last exposure. If they do not get the disease after twelve days, they are allowed to go back to school.

Children with measles must usually be kept out of school from the beginning of the disease until the rash has disappeared. And children with mumps are often isolated from the beginning of the disease until all swelling has disappeared.

Local health departments usually follow the regulations of the provincial Department of Health for checking the spread of communicable diseases.

These regulations have changed somewhat in recent years. For example, children with chicken pox, German measles, and mumps are not now isolated in all communities. There is a trend toward discontinuing isolation for these three minor diseases because it has been found that isolation hasn't helped much to check the spread of them.

After the close of a patient's period of isolation, the health department sees that the patient's room and furniture are *disinfected,* or cleansed of any harmful germs. Usually the health department nurse explains how to do this. The room, with all its furnishings, is disinfected by being thoroughly washed with soap and hot water. The room is then aired and plenty of sunlight is allowed to enter. Up-to-date health departments no longer use *fumigation* to disinfect a room.

WHAT YOU AND YOUR FAMILY CAN DO

As you can see, public health departments do a great deal to help keep communicable diseases from spreading. But *you* can help, too.

One thing you can do is to be sure you have had vaccinations and inoculations that keep you from getting diseases like smallpox and diphtheria.

Another thing you and your family can do is to call a doctor if there is reason to think that someone in the family has a communicable disease. If your family should be placed in quarantine, all the members should obey the rules.

If an *epidemic,* or a number of cases of a communicable disease, breaks out, you should follow the directions given by your health department.

218

In the pictures above, you can see all those in the community who were especially concerned when Joe Fuller became ill with scarlet fever. What should each do to keep the disease from spreading?

Now can you describe some of the things that might happen if any of the persons shown above did not do his part to check the spread of the disease?

THE COMMUNITY WATER SUPPLY

"Isn't it funny!" said Allen when his class began studying how his town got its water supply. "I've been turning on a tap and getting a drink for a long time, but I never before wondered very much about where the water comes from."

"I've suddenly begun to wonder about a lot of things," said Elizabeth. "I know the water comes into our taps through pipes, but where do the pipes come from? And how does the health department test the water to see if it is safe?"

After these and other questions had been raised, Miss Thompson's class set out to find all the information they could about their community's water supply.

WHERE THE WATER COMES FROM

First of all, the class learned that a very important problem all municipalities face is the one of supplying people with water for drinking and for household purposes. Many places get their water from nearby lakes or rivers. But sometimes they use artesian wells or build huge storage places, or *reservoirs,* to save water that flows into them from streams and to store it for use.

Winnipeg, for example, brings its water in by pipes from Shoal Lake, about ninety miles to the east of the city.

The children learned that their own town of Williston gets its water from Fish Lake, a large lake about five miles south of town.

The water is brought to Williston, as it is brought to other towns and cities, through pipes that are laid underground. As the water is taken into these pipes, coarse screens are used to keep fish, leaves, and sticks from entering.

HOW THE WATER IS MADE PURE

As is most often the case, the pipes that bring water to Williston lead to the town waterworks. Here the water is first treated with a chemical called *alum*, and then it is filtered.

As the water filters through the layers of sand and gravel, dirt of all kinds is filtered out

WATER

SAND

GRAVEL

After the water filters down through layers of sand and gravel into the underdrains shown in the picture on page 221, it looks clean. But there may still be some harmful germs, or bacteria, in it, and therefore it is treated with another chemical called *chlorine*. The chlorine kills bacteria and makes the water safe to drink.

Of course, not all cities and towns treat their water in exactly this way to make it pure. Some cities that get their water from wells or from surface supplies do not filter the water, but they almost always put chlorine or other chemicals in it. Some of the solid materials settle out of the water while it is stored in the reservoirs, but chemicals are needed to destroy the harmful bacteria.

The chief ways that communities make the water supply pure are (1) by filtering it and (2) by adding chemicals, such as chlorine, to it.

After the water has been made safe for use, it is carried by pipes to the different houses and apartments in the town or city.

In the picture at the top of page 223, you can see how water is pumped into Allen's house through the town's pipe lines.

Follow the path that the water takes from the pipe lines to the kitchen sink.

When Allen turns on the tap at the sink, water comes out of the pipe. It is forced out by the pressure of the pumps at the waterworks, which are continually pumping water into the pipe lines.

When Allen turns off the tap, a little valve in the pipe keeps the water from flowing out.

Can you tell from the picture above how the water in Allen's house is heated?

HOW DRINKING WATER IS TESTED

Allen's class learned that from time to time the health officer in their community takes samples of the drinking water from Williston to the Department of Health. Here the laboratory workers test it to be sure that it is safe. *Safe drinking water does not have the kinds of bacteria in it that cause diseases such as typhoid fever.*

In large communities the local health department has its own laboratory workers to test the water to make certain it is safe for drinking. Some water departments also have their own laboratories for testing water, or use branch laboratories of the provincial Department of Health.

If a laboratory test should show that the drinking water is not safe, the water should be boiled until some other measures can be taken to make sure that it *is* safe.

HOW COUNTRY HOMES GET WATER

While they were studying how their community gets its water supply, Allen's class also learned how people living in small villages or on farms get their water. These people have no town or city water system to pipe in safe water, and they usually get water from wells in their own yards.

People using water from their own wells should have the water tested often. This can be done by sending samples in special containers to the provincial Department of Health. If there is any question about the safety of the water, it should be boiled before it is used.

Wells should be lined with pipe casings. They should be placed on high ground and should be sunk down below the water level—deep enough so that water comes from an area free of pollution. This must be done to prevent drainage from barn lots or outdoor toilets from seeping into the wells.

Layer of rock or clay

Water level

You have been learning the ways by which different communities get their water and make it safe for drinking.

Now see if you can answer these questions about your *own* community.

Does your community get its water from a lake or river, from reservoirs, or from wells?

How is the water in your community made safe?

If you don't know the answers to these questions, where can you find the information?

You should keep in mind, of course, that it isn't enough to make sure that safe water is pumped into your homes and into your school. You must be careful to keep it safe.

For example, you should use your own drinking glass or a fresh paper cup. Why is this important?

When you are using a public drinking fountain, you should be careful to keep your mouth off the fountain itself. Why?

When you are on a hike you may need to drink water from a spring or well. What should you do if you are not sure that the water is pure?

Why is it a good plan to carry a canteen when you are hiking?

HOW SEWAGE IS CARRIED AWAY

After learning how water is pumped into their homes, the boys and girls in Miss Thompson's class next wanted to know what happens to *used water,* such as dishwater and bathwater.

After investigating, they learned that *used water, together with wastes from human bodies, is called sewage and is carried away through the town's sewerage system.*

In the town of Williston, as in other towns and cities with public water systems, the sewage is carried from the homes in pipes which lead to larger sewer lines buried under the streets.

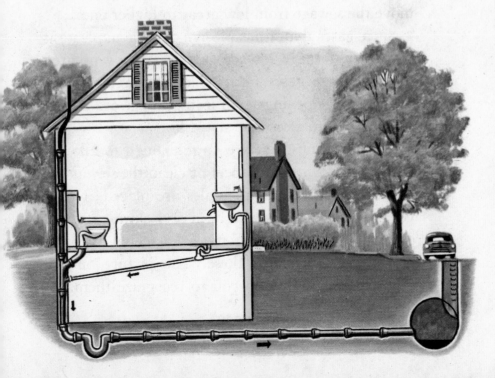

In Williston these sewer lines, which are often called *laterals,* also drain off the rain water that collects in the streets. Some cities, however, have separate rain-water sewers, and these cities are not so likely to have their sewer pipes choked up in times of heavy rainfall.

When sewer pipes get overloaded, sewage may "back up" into basements and flood them. This sometimes happens in Williston.

The sewer pipes in Williston, as in many towns, are sloped just enough to keep the sewage flowing along steadily until it gets to the town's sewage-treatment plant. Some cities also use pumps to move the sewage from low areas to higher ones.

Since gases that are explosive or have unpleasant odors may form in sewers, the sewers are ventilated to keep these gases from collecting in the pipes. That is why openings with iron gratings are placed here and there along the sewer lines.

These gratings that are large enough to allow a man to go down and inspect or clean the sewers are called *manholes.* Such manholes are placed at convenient places for examination and cleaning. Look carefully on your way home from school and you may see gratings like these. The picture on the opposite page will help you to recognize them.

Storm water inlet

Manhole

Not all the gas or odor that forms in the sewers comes out through the manholes in the sewer system. Some of it may back up into the pipes leading to homes. This gas does not cause disease, but the odor is unpleasant. To protect homes from this odor, sinks and washbowls have a bend, or trap, in the pipe. This part of the pipe holds enough water at all times to keep such odors from entering the house.

Traps that keep sewer gas from backing up into the house

Emptying sewage into lakes, rivers, and streams is a common way of getting rid of it. The town of Williston empties its sewage into the Sandy River, which flows near the edge of town. But before sewage is emptied, it must be treated to destroy the bacteria and to prevent a nuisance.

On page 231 you can see some important parts of the Williston *sewage-treatment plant*. Such plants differ in various towns and cities. *But the purpose of all sewage-treatment plants is to purify the sewage.* An important duty of the health department is to see that this is done.

In the Williston plant the sewage first passes through a screen of metal bars which catches large particles that might clog the sewer pumps. The sewage then flows into a shallow, concrete channel called a *grit chamber*. Here the sewage is slowed down and the heavier particles, such as grit and sand, settle to the bottom.

Next the sewage flows into a settling tank. You can see a picture of a settling tank on page 231. Here the sewage moves more slowly, so that the floating particles can settle to the bottom. This settled material is called *sludge*.

From the settling tank the sewage is carried to another tank for further treatment. One kind of tank used for this purpose is a bed of stones six feet deep. The sewage is sprayed onto the stones, where it flows downward. The bacteria and solid particles cling to the stones until finally they form thick coatings which peel off and are carried away with the liquid.

To remove these coatings, the sewage is passed through a final settling tank, where the coatings

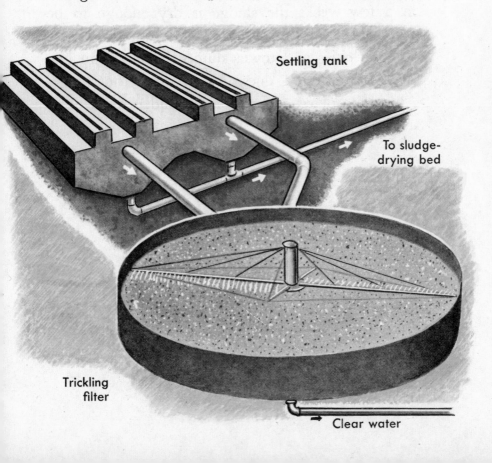

Settling tank

To sludge-drying bed

Trickling filter

Clear water

settle to the bottom. From this tank the liquid sewage flows through pipes into the river.

Sludge from the final settling tank is pumped back to a storage tank called a *digester*. Here the sludge loses its unpleasant odor. Then it is passed along to *sludge-drying beds* like the ones shown below. In Williston these beds are open ones, but in some cities they are enclosed.

In the sludge-drying beds most of the moisture is removed through drainage and evaporation. Then in a few weeks the sludge is dry enough to be shovelled up and taken for final disposal.

Some cities and towns dump the sludge in low areas as Williston does. A few burn the sludge. And some places get rid of the sludge by using it as a fertilizer.

Sludge-drying beds

Homes that have running water and are connected with a public sewer system have few problems in getting rid of sewage. But farm and village homes have a much greater problem.

If the home has running water but is not connected with a public sewer system, wastes may be piped into a *septic tank* buried outside.

A septic tank is built so that the solid material in the sewage sinks to the bottom of the tank. Here the action of certain bacteria breaks up the material and makes it odorless. The water from the sewage is drained away by pipes which carry it into the ground. A septic tank should usually be cleaned once in two or three years.

If there is no running water in a house, used water, such as dishwater and bathwater, should be discharged into a leaching well or cesspit or passed out into the ground through pipes similar to those from a septic tank. But human wastes are usually taken care of through outdoor toilets.

One kind of outdoor toilet is built over an open pit in which waste is collected. The waste is removed from time to time and the pit disinfected, or the toilet is moved to a new pit and the old one is covered up.

Another kind of outdoor toilet is built over a tank which can be removed and emptied when necessary. Daily use of chlorinated lime can keep this toilet and the kind built over a pit from being objectionable. Still another kind has a watertight tank, and a strong chemical is used in the tank to destroy odors and disease-carrying bacteria, or it may operate like a septic tank. This tank must be emptied from time to time. All outdoor toilets should be proof against flies.

SEWAGE IN YOUR COMMUNITY

If there is a public sewerage system in your town or city, can you answer these questions about it?

What evidences of the sewerage system can you see as you walk along the street?

Where is the sewage-treatment plant, if any?

Where is the sewage emptied after being treated?

What does the sewage-treatment plant do with sludge from the sludge-drying beds?

How might you learn the answers to questions about the sewerage system in your town?

If there is no sewerage system where you live, describe how the sewage in your home is taken care of. What precautions should be taken with the method used in your home?

GARBAGE AND RUBBISH

Allen and his classmates wanted to know how garbage and rubbish were taken care of in Williston. So they chose Kenneth as head of a committee to find out about this problem.

Kenneth decided to talk to the garbage collectors, who came to pick up the garbage each Monday morning. The following Monday, when he saw the garbage truck pull into the alley behind the school, he hurried out to talk to the men.

Later he told the others what he had found out.

"The garbage truck takes the garbage out to the dump yard at the edge of town," he reported. "The garbage, ashes, tin cans, and bottles are all dumped there in big piles."

"Is that all you found out?" exclaimed Allen.

"I haven't finished," Kenneth answered. "The men said that people in Williston aren't satisfied with the way the garbage is being taken care of and neither is the health department. They think it ought to be collected more often. And people who live near the dump say it smells bad and is a breeding place for flies and rats.

"The collectors said our town council is talking about better ways of getting rid of the garbage. Before long the council may pass some new laws to see that the garbage is taken care of properly."

"Say!" said Bill Fulton. "My uncle is on the council. I'll ask him to tell me some better ways that Williston might use to get rid of garbage."

So Bill asked his uncle, and a few days later he brought in a booklet his uncle had given him.

On pages 237, 238, and 239 you can see some pages from this booklet. Study them until *you* can tell about some ways of collecting garbage and disposing of it that are better than the method Williston used.

COLLECTION OF GARBAGE

To be satisfactory, a city garbage-collection service should be regular and should cover the entire city. Garbage should be collected at least once a week and oftener in summer because bad odors and flies and rats increase then.

CITY-OWNED GARBAGE CANS

An excellent collection method is the one in which the city owns all garbage cans and furnishes them to homes, stores, hotels, and restaurants. When a collection is made, the filled can is loaded on the truck and a clean, empty can is left in its place. This method makes sure that tightly covered, clean cans are used everywhere. It is a method that keeps rats and flies from being too troublesome. It is an expensive method, however.

PRIVATELY OWNED CONTAINERS

When people provide their own containers, the city should require that metal cans with tight lids be used— and that all cans be kept as clean as possible.

DISPOSAL OF GARBAGE

CITY-OWNED INCINERATOR

This is an excellent method, but it re-
quires the city or town to build an incinerator. Most small towns cannot afford this
method, but many big cities use it. However, this method will not take care of
glass, metal, and ashes. So rubbish of that
kind must be disposed of in some other
way.

KITCHEN GRINDER

Some people can afford to place a special grinder under the sinks
in their kitchens. These grinders grind up all the garbage so it can go
through the used-water pipes and into the city sewer system.

Grinders are a fine way of taking care of garbage.

SANITARY LAND FILL

This is a new and in many ways a very satisfactory method of taking care of garbage and rubbish. It is a method used by the army in wartime. Any city, any size, can use it.

With this method, a tractor digs a trench at the dump yard. Garbage and rubbish are hauled in and dumped into one end of the trench. A bull-and-clam shovel on the tractor pushes down on the layers of garbage. This flattens all cans, breaks all glass into bits, and leaves no air space. At the end of each day, the garbage is covered with earth which the tractor digs up when making a new trench for use on the next day.

This method leaves no unpleasant-looking dump piles and no garbage or rubbish to attract mice, rats, cockroaches, or flies. It also does away with the bad odors that come from the open dump yards.

How are garbage and rubbish taken care of in your community?

Do you think your community uses the best way of taking care of its garbage? What improvements could you suggest in your community's method?

Of course, even if your community takes most of the responsibility for getting rid of the garbage, there are things *you* and your family can do to help. You can wrap your garbage and have it ready to be picked up on collection days. You can try to provide a metal can with a tight lid, and you can keep the garbage can as clean as possible. Why is a tight lid important? A clean can?

If you live on a farm or in a small village, you and your family may have all the responsibility for taking care of the garbage. You may feed some of it to hogs. However, only garbage that is *cooked* should be used in this way. Other garbage may be buried, or your family may use its own incinerator for burning the garbage. Rubbish, such as tin cans and ashes, may be either buried or burned.

Whatever methods are used, care should be taken to dispose of garbage *regularly*.

FIGHTING FLIES AND RATS

While they were finding out how their community takes care of its sewage and garbage, the boys and girls in Kenneth's class discovered that getting rid of such pests as flies and rats is a community problem, too.

The class sent for some booklets that explained ways of fighting flies and rats and that told *why* it is so important that these pests be controlled. The material below is from one of these booklets and it gives some suggestions for getting rid of rats and flies. What are the suggestions?

Flies and Rats are a Menace!

DON'T ENCOURAGE THEM......FIGHT THEM

If you don't leave food, rubbish, and garbage around, you can help starve out the rats and discourage the flies.

Keep all garbage in tightly covered containers.

In summer, use screens on windows and doors of your home to keep out flies. Be sure to use screens on doors and windows of outside toilets.

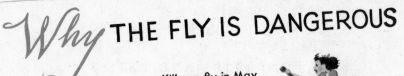 Why THE FLY IS DANGEROUS

Kill one fly in May and you'll keep many away!

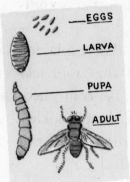

EGGS

LARVA

PUPA

ADULT

LIFE CYCLE OF A FLY

In a single summer ten or twelve generations of flies may develop and mature. That's why it's necessary to start fighting flies as soon as they begin to appear and before they can breed thousands more.

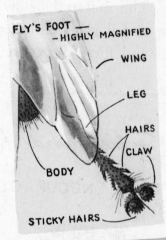

FLY'S FOOT — —HIGHLY MAGNIFIED

WING

LEG

HAIRS

CLAW

BODY

STICKY HAIRS

Flies like filth. They walk in garbage, manure, and rubbish. Then with their feet covered with filth and germs, they come into our homes and even walk on our food, IF WE AREN'T CAREFUL.

Flies can spread the germs of typhoid fever, intestinal diseases, and tuberculosis.

The material above gives some reasons why flies are a nuisance and are dangerous to have around. What are some of the reasons?

Why THE RAT IS DANGEROUS

The health of a community is always in danger when rats are around. Rats can spread typhus fever and another disease called the plague.

Rats are very destructive and cause millions of dollars' damage every year.

Rats feed upon eggs, poultry, fruits, and vegetables in homes and stores if such foods are not properly protected. They also destroy grain in the fields.

Rats have also been known to cause fires by gnawing on matches or on the coverings of electric wires.

Nowadays many houses and stores are built so that they are rat-proof. And at our seaports special rat guards, like round tin collars, are fitted over the ropes that tie ships to the docks. These guards keep rats from coming ashore or going onto the ships.

This material gives some reasons why rats are dangerous. What are the reasons?

What can *your* community do to fight flies and rats? What can *you* and your family do?

243

In the material that Miss Thompson's class received from the local health department were some explanations about the food inspections made in food stores, bakeries, restaurants, ice-cream parlors, meat markets, and other places where food is made or sold. Inspections like these are made by health departments in communities to be sure that foods are healthful and to prevent the spread of disease through foods.

Restaurants, food stores, bakeries, and food factories of all kinds must have permission from the town or city to operate. This permission is usually granted in the form of a *licence* which can be posted on the wall for display.

Before a licence is granted to them, all places that make or sell food must be inspected by the local health department. And after they have been granted a licence, these places are inspected regularly to be sure they are maintaining proper standards of cleanliness—standards that are set up by the local health department.

When they are inspecting a food store or a restaurant, the inspectors look first to see if the workers in the store are clean.

Next they look to see if the surroundings are clean—clean floors, clean shelves, clean storage places, and clean washrooms.

The inspectors also watch the workers to see if they follow the important rules that all food handlers should observe. These rules are:

1. Always wash your hands thoroughly with soap and hot water and dry them on a clean towel before handling food and right after using a handkerchief or going to the toilet. *This rule is most important in helping prevent the spread of disease through food by careless food handlers.*

2. Avoid preparing or handling foods if you have a sore throat or if you have sores or infected cuts on your hands, arms, or face.

3. Wash dishes, silverware, glasses, and all cooking utensils properly. This means washing the dishes in plenty of hot, soapy water; changing the dishwater often; and rinsing dishes with boiling water. In some cities, restaurants are also required to use steam for disinfectant or to add proper amounts of chemicals to the rinsing water to help kill germs on dishes and other eating utensils.

In some meat markets, the inspectors check to be sure that all meat sold at the market has been stamped or examined by the meat-inspection department.

In food stores and restaurants, the inspectors pay special attention to the handling and storing of such foods as cream-puff fillings, custards, milk, soup, cooked spaghetti and macaroni, sandwich fillings, and creamed dishes. Bacteria are most likely to grow in moist foods of this kind. That is why these foods must be given particular care.

If these foods are not all used up the day that they are freshly prepared, they should be stored in clean, *cold* places; and they should not be kept too long. Restaurants are warned that it is better to throw away leftover foods of this kind if they have been standing in a warm place for some time, or if they have been kept too long, especially in warm weather.

Of course, a food store or restaurant that *looks* clean may not always be as safe as it looks. For example, the dishes and silverware in a restaurant may seem to be very clean, but if they have been improperly washed or carelessly handled these utensils may still have too many bacteria on them to be safe.

That is why health departments make *swab tests* on eating and drinking utensils in restaurants and other eating places.

To make a swab test the health officer uses a small piece of cotton which has been specially prepared for the test. This piece of cotton is known as a swab. The health officer passes the swab carefully around the rim of a drinking glass or other eating utensil. Then he drops it into a germ-free container and sends it to the health-department laboratory.

At the laboratory a count is made of the bacteria that were taken from the eating utensil. If the bacterial count is too high, the owner of the eating place is warned that eating utensils must be more carefully washed.

As you have learned, every community should try to see that all food made or sold in it is safe.

What are some things *your* community does to see that the food you and your family buy is safe?

How can you learn more about how your community protects your food?

Have you noticed any licences posted in the food stores or restaurants of your community?

What is the meaning of these licences?

Have you noticed the blue stamp on the meats you buy? What is the meaning of this stamp?

Do you know how you can help your local health department in its work of keeping food stores and eating places safe and clean? One thing you can do is to buy only at clean and sanitary places.

Of course, you can't expect your community to do all the work of protecting your food. After the food comes into your home, you and your family must keep it clean and safe.

What precautions in storing foods should be taken in your home? In washing dishes and cooking utensils? In handling leftovers such as custards and creamed dishes? In making fresh fruits, such as apples, pears, and peaches, safe for eating?

SAFEGUARDING THE MILK

To learn more about how the milk in their town was made safe for use, the boys and girls in Miss Thompson's class made a trip to the Harris Dairy in Williston.

At the dairy Mr. Harris, the owner, talked to the class for a while before he showed them through the plant.

"Milk is a very important food," Mr. Harris explained. "Great quantities of it are used here in Williston and in every other community. But, while milk is an important food, it can also be a dangerous food unless care is taken to keep it clean and to keep all harmful bacteria out of it."

Mr. Harris went on to explain that bacteria grow very easily in milk—and that while some of these bacteria are harmless, others can cause such diseases as typhoid fever, tuberculosis, and septic sore throat.

"Every possible care must be taken to keep the milk in a sanitary condition from the time it is taken from the cows until it is placed in bottles or paper containers and delivered," he said.

Then Mr. Harris described what happened to the milk before it was delivered to his dairy. He said that the milk was brought by trucks from dairy farms in the neighborhood and that all of these farms had been carefully inspected by the health department.

"Milk is warm when it comes from the cow," Mr. Harris said, "and warm milk always provides

Cleanliness is important on a dairy farm. Barns must be kept clean. Workers must wear clean clothing and wash their hands before each milking. Milk pails must be sterilized. Any machinery must be cleaned daily.

Health inspectors check to see if the cows are healthy, if they are handled by healthy farm workers, and if they have been given tuberculin tests to see if they carry the germs of tuberculosis.

Which methods would be used in transporting milk long distances?

a good place for bacteria to grow. That is why the milk is taken at once to a milk house, where it is strained and poured into large cans which have been sterilized. The cans of milk are then stored in a cool place, where they are kept at a temperature of about 50 degrees until they are ready to be sent away to the dairy."

Mr. Harris also mentioned that in large cities milk often comes from dairy farms as far away as one or two hundred miles. In situations like these the milk is taken to the dairies in special trucks or in express milk trains. The trucks and the tank cars of the train are designed to keep the milk at a temperature of 50 degrees or less. You can see a milk truck and a milk tank car in the picture at the top of this page.

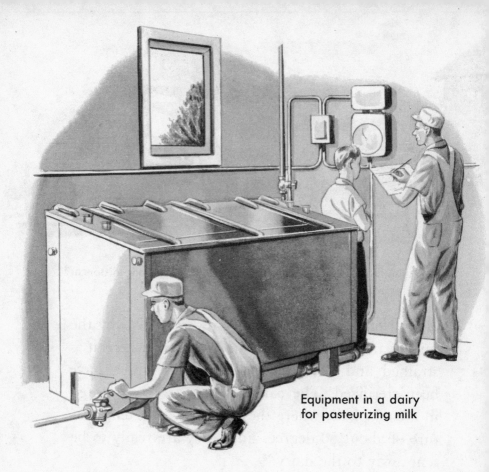

Equipment in a dairy
for pasteurizing milk

After explaining how the milk got to his dairy, Mr. Harris took the class on a tour through the dairy. One of the most important things the boys and girls saw was the equipment for *pasteurizing* milk, which you can see in the picture above. *Pasteurizing is a process all dairies use to destroy harmful bacteria that might cause dangerous diseases.*

The usual method of pasteurizing milk is to heat it to a temperature of from 142 to 145 degrees and keep it at this temperature for at least half an hour. Sometimes, however, the quick method of pasteurizing is used. With this method, the milk is heated to a temperature of from 160 to 165 degrees and kept at that temperature for 15 or 16 seconds.

After the milk has been pasteurized, it is quickly cooled to a temperature of 50 degrees or lower and kept at that temperature until it is bottled and ready for delivery.

The machinery that was used in Mr. Harris' dairy to bottle the milk was quite fascinating to Allen and the others. This machinery cleaned the bottles, sterilized them, filled them with pasteurized milk, and capped them tightly.

This machinery cleans, fills, and caps the bottles—without any help from human hands.

From reading about the trip Allen and his classmates made to a local dairy, you have learned some important things a community does to safeguard its milk supply. What are some of these things?

If you could make a trip to a dairy farm, what things would you want to see and ask about?

What would you want to see and inquire about if you could visit a dairy in your community?

Even if you can't make trips such as these, there are some very important things you can learn about your milk by reading what is printed on the milk-bottle cap or on a paper milk container.

For example, look at the material printed on this milk container.

Has this milk been pasteurized?

Does it contain vitamin D?

What other information is given?

Some milk is skimmed and then enriched with vitamins A and D.

254

Do you know what the word *homogenized* means? It means that the milk has been treated so that the cream remains mixed with the milk instead of rising to the top. Is the milk you usually drink homogenized? How do you know?

Of course, homogenized milk has some disadvantages. Sometimes a doctor orders a patient to drink *skim milk,* which is milk that has no butterfat in it. If the milk has not been homogenized, this skim milk can easily be obtained. It is the milk left in the bottle after the cream, which has risen to the top, has been poured off.

Do you know how your health department checks your milk supply to be sure it is safe? In addition to inspecting dairy farms and dairies, the health department regularly collects samples of milk from stores and delivery wagons and sends these samples to the laboratory to be tested.

Of course, there are things *you* can do, too, to keep your milk safe. If it is delivered, you can bring it in promptly from your doorstep. You can wash the top before milk is poured from the container. You can store milk in a cool place and you can avoid using it after it has been kept too long. Why are all these precautions important?

What precautions do *you* take with milk?

What Do You Think?

1. Little Johnnie Smith had a fever and a rash, and his mother decided to call the doctor right away. "I think Johnnie is getting scarlet fever," she said.

"Oh my, Mother," cried Johnnie's sister, Paula. *"Don't* call a doctor. If Johnnie has scarlet fever, the doctor will quarantine us. And I don't want to be shut up like that!"

Would you like to have Paula for a neighbor in your community? Why or why not?

What advice could you give Paula to convince her of the importance of calling the doctor?

 2. "Say, Jack," said Bill one day. "If you try, you can get all your garbage in the metal can. Pack it down. Then you won't have to use that old paper box for garbage."

"Why don't you mind your own business?" Jack snapped. "What I do with our garbage is none of your affair!"

Is it true that what one family does with its garbage is of no concern to other families in the neighborhood? What makes you think as you do?

3. "Here's a clear spring," said Sam when he and some friends were on a hike. "You can tell just by looking at it that the water is safe to drink."

Can you tell "just by looking at it" whether water is safe for drinking? Why or why not?

What might you find near a well or spring to tell you the water is safe to drink?

What should you do if you are not sure whether water is safe for drinking?

4. Thelma read in the paper that the mayors of all cities were urged to appoint citizens' committees to plan ways of controlling rats. "My goodness," she thought. "I'd think that mayors would have more important things to do than worry about rats!"

Do you think rats are a problem important enough to take up the attention of the mayor and other citizens? What makes you think so?

5. After communities in this country made laws about pure water and milk supplies and about proper disposal of sewage and garbage, fewer and fewer people in the communities died of communicable diseases.

How do you explain the connection between better laws about community sanitation and fewer deaths from communicable diseases?

"Health Heroes"

When the Health Exhibit took place, the people in Williston were interested in seeing the various displays the children had prepared.

The posters that Allen's class had made attracted quite a bit of attention. And so did another set of "Quiz" posters about health heroes that a seventh-grade class had made. You can see these posters on page 259.

After trying to guess who the men on these posters were, Allen and Kenneth and some of their classmates asked Miss Thompson for help. "How can we find out the names of all the men on the posters?" they asked.

"There are some books in the library that will help you," Miss Thompson replied.

"Just what *is* a health hero?" asked Kenneth.

"Well," said Miss Thompson, "the easiest way to explain a health hero is to say he is a doctor or scientist or some other person who has made a discovery or found a new treatment that has helped in the battle against disease."

Then she went on to explain that people living in communities a long time ago were not always so healthy as they are today.

A___ V__ L___
1632 ★ 1723

E___ J___
1749 ★ 1823

L___ P___
1822 ★ 1895

J___ L___
1827 ★ 1912

R__ K___
1843 ★ 1910

W__ R___
1851 ★ 1902

Can You Name These Men?

YOU AND YOUR COMMUNITY ARE SAFER TODAY BECAUSE OF THESE
HEALTH HEROES OF YESTERDAY

She also explained that it is only within the past one hundred years or so that people have known much about communicable diseases.

"Before that time," she said, "the death rate from communicable diseases was very, very high. Epidemics of such diseases as typhoid fever, smallpox, diphtheria, cholera, and yellow fever were common; and hundreds of thousands of people died from them. Unfortunately, no one knew much about the cause or treatment of these diseases.

"For example, until a hundred and fifty years ago or thereabouts, everyone expected to have smallpox sometime during his lifetime, and one person in every twelve died from it. But in the years since that time great progress has been made in discovering the causes of communicable diseases and in learning how to treat and prevent them."

Then Miss Thompson mentioned that the men shown on page 259 had all made important contributions to man's progress in fighting disease.

"These men made some of the early and very important discoveries," she said. "But many other men, less well known, aided, too. And in recent years other great discoveries such as the 'wonder drugs,' *penicillin* and *sulfa*, have resulted from the work of modern health heroes."

Later, the children were looking through some reference books. This is some of the information they found about the men in the "Quiz" posters.

ANTON VAN LEEUWENHOEK

About the time the first settlers were coming to America, Anton van Leeuwenhoek was born in Holland. When he grew up, he earned his living as a janitor of the Town Hall. But he also had a hobby, that of making microscopes and using them to look at all sorts of things.

He kept making better and better microscopes until at last, in 1675, he had one so strong that when he looked into a drop of rain water, he could see what he called "little animals" in it. Although he did not know it, some of these "little animals" were germs. As a result of Van Leeuwenhoek's work, Louis Pasteur was aided some two hundred years later in proving that germs cause diseases.

EDWARD JENNER

This man was a country doctor in England. In the year 1796 he made medical history by proving that he could protect people from smallpox. Jenner did this by putting into people's skin a tiny bit of fluid from a sore caused by cowpox, which is a mild disease of cows.

This method of protecting people from small-pox was called "vaccination." It was a very good protection from the disease, but not even Jenner knew why the vaccination worked.

It wasn't until the year 1879 that Louis Pasteur discovered why vaccinations work. The reason is this: In fighting the weak germs of a disease which are placed in the body through vaccination, the body manufactures *antibodies* which protect it against the strong germs of a similar disease.

LOUIS PASTEUR

Until the time of Louis Pasteur, people had no idea of what caused communicable diseases. Many men had puzzled over the cause, but the scientist Pasteur found the answer.

Although he made many discoveries, such as the fact that heat will kill bacteria, Pasteur's most important work was to prove that each kind of communicable disease is caused by a special kind of germ which enters the body from the outside. When living germs get inside the body, the warmth and moisture and food there aid their growth. As the germs eat and live in the body, they throw off poisons. These poisons make a person feel sick when he has a disease caused by germs.

While Pasteur was doing his important work in France, an English doctor named Joseph Lister was trying to discover why so many people died from infections after being wounded.

In 1865, Lister read some writings of Louis Pasteur which made him think that germs could enter the body through openings made by wounds. To test his idea, he used *carbolic acid* to kill germs around the wounds. Then he noted that such wounds no longer became infected.

Next Lister began to use a solution of carbolic acid to wash his hands and his instruments before he operated on patients. He also used this solution on the dressings applied after an operation. Soon other doctors began to follow Lister's example.

ROBERT KOCH

Robert Koch was a country doctor in Germany who also became interested in Pasteur's studies. He began to grow bacteria in his laboratory and to study them through his microscope. After a while, he thought of putting gelatin into a broth. The bacteria in the broth then grew on the surface of the gelatin, and it was easier to study them.

Robert Koch is often called the father of *bacteriology*, which is the scientific study of bacteria. He is also known to the world as the man who first discovered the causes of tuberculosis and suggested a way of checking it.

WALTER REED

In June of the year 1900, Walter Reed and a group of other doctors were sent by the United States government to Cuba to try to find ways of fighting yellow fever.

After much study, Dr. Reed and his helpers decided that the disease might be spread by mosquitoes. Experiments were carried on during which the doctors with Reed, as well as some United States soldiers, allowed themselves to be bitten by mosquitoes—mosquitoes which had earlier filled themselves with the blood of yellow-fever patients. In several days those who had been bitten also became ill with the disease.

As a result of these and many other experiments, Walter Reed and those who worked with him proved that yellow fever is carried by a certain kind of mosquito. Once the cause of the disease was known, breeding places of mosquitoes were cleaned up, and the disease almost wiped out.

THIS COMMUNITY IS WHAT YOU MAKE IT!

What Are **You** Doing to Make It A Safer, Pleasanter Healthier Place In Which To Live?

Your Community — and You

For their part in the Health Exhibit at school the boys and girls in one of the eighth-grade classes made a dozen or more posters like the one above. They placed the posters in the bus station, in the bank, and in store windows, as well as in the main hall of their school.

Miss Thompson thought the poster shown above was such a good one that she borrowed it one morning so that the boys and girls in her class could think about it and discuss it thoroughly.

Below, you can see what Allen and some of his classmates said in answer to the question about what could be done to make the community *safer*.

What can *you* do to make your community a safer place in which to live?

Obey traffic signals. Be sure not to "jaywalk."

Play in safe places . . . not in streets and alleys.

Follow the safety code for bicycle riders.

Check your house often to be sure there are no hazards, such as worn electric cords or old paper in the attic or basement.

Be careful on buses and in cars. Keep your hands and head safely inside the window.

If it's icy, make your porch and sidewalks safe by putting sand or ashes on them.

At first Allen and Jane and their classmates were puzzled about how to answer the question, "What can you do to make your community a *pleasanter* place in which to live?"

So Miss Thompson gave them a hint. "When we are in a city park, we ought to be as careful and as tidy as we would be at home," she said. "For example, we wouldn't throw old cans and boxes on our floors at home and leave them there. But too often we are careless and do that after picnics in the park. Instead we should throw our rubbish into the rubbish containers just as we would do at home."

After that the boys and girls thought of other suggestions. Some of their suggestions about making their community pleasanter were:

1. Treat public property as carefully as you treat your own belongings at home.

2. Treat others courteously. Don't push or crowd or shout on buses and streetcars, in stores, or in other public places.

3. Be friendly. Smile and say "hello" when you meet your neighbors. Try to make newcomers in the neighborhood feel welcome.

What other suggestions can *you* offer about ways to make your community a pleasanter place in which to live?

After talking over ways of making the community a *healthier* place in which to live, Kenneth and Allen and the others made cartoons showing some of their best suggestions. As you can see below and on the next page, their cartoons all showed ways of avoiding the spread of disease germs.

THAT SNEEZE CAN SEND DROP-
LETS CONTAINING COLD GERMS
AND OTHER BACTERIA A
DISTANCE OF 12 FEET OR MORE.

DON'T SPREAD GERMS IF
YOU CAN HELP IT.
CATCH YOUR COUGHS AND
SNEEZES IN A HANDKERCHIEF.

SPITTING CAN SPREAD GERMS!
YOU WOULDN'T SPIT ON YOUR
FLOOR AT HOME, SO DON'T
DO IT OUT IN PUBLIC.

UNCOVERED GARBAGE BRINGS
RATS AND FLIES.
KEEP YOUR GARBAGE IN TIGHTLY
COVERED CONTAINERS!

PROTECT YOURSELF AND
PROTECT OTHERS. KEEP
YOUR MOUTH OFF THE
DRINKING FOUNTAIN!

IF YOU DON'T PATRONIZE
UNCLEAN STORES AND
EATING PLACES, THEY WILL
BE FORCED TO CLEAN UP!

What other ways can *you* suggest for helping
to keep germs from spreading in your community?

Avoiding the spread of germs that can cause disease is, of course, very important in making your community a healthier place in which to live. But there is something else you can do, too. *You can make every effort to keep yourself in the best possible physical condition.* For a truly healthy community is one in which as many people as possible are in excellent physical condition and so are able to *resist,* or fight, germs that cause disease.

Below and on the next page you can see and review once more the important guides for healthful living.

Be ready to explain why each of these guides is essential in building and maintaining good health.

Have a physical examination once a year or as often as your doctor thinks is necessary.

why? _____

Keep your teeth clean and in good repair. See your dentist once every six months or as often as he advises you.

why? _____

Eat a well-balanced diet each day
—try to follow Canada's Food Rules,
shown in the picture on page 127 of
this book.

why?

Keep your muscles strong.
Whenever possible, spend an
hour or more each day working or playing outdoors.

why?

Get ten hours of sleep each
night, except on very special
occasions. Learn to relax now
and then during the day.

why?

Work for happy feelings
most of the time. WHAT ARE
SOME WAYS TO DO THIS?

why?

The last of these guides is sometimes neglected.
Yet it is very important because your body works
more efficiently when you are happy and relaxed
than when you are unhappy or anxious. And your
good health depends not only upon having medical and dental check-ups and on getting adequate
sleep, exercise, and diet. It also depends upon
having happy feelings and upon knowing how
to get along with yourself—and with others.

Things for You to Think About

1. Many communities have a law forbidding cars to go over thirty miles an hour within the city limits.

Do you think such a law helps make a community safer? What makes you think so? What else besides speeding can cause accidents in which persons are hit by cars? How can such accidents be prevented?

2. Some communities forbid the sale of alcoholic drinks within the limits of the community.

Might this law help make a community safer? Why do you think as you do?

3. A book Jean was reading said, "Progress in community health is the result of the work of many men from many nations."

Do you think this statement is correct? Why?

4. Joe said, "I can name the health heroes on page 259, and I can tell what each man did."

Can you do this, too?

5. It has sometimes been said that "people are no safer than the community in which they live, and a community is no safer than the people who live in it."

What do you think this statement means?

Things for You to Do

1. Many other people besides the ones shown on page 259 have helped in the war against disease. Some of them are: Wilhelm Roentgen, William Harvey, Florence Nightingale, Bela Schick, Pierre and Marie Curie, and Sir Frederick Banting.

Use the encyclopedia or other reference books to learn about these and other health heroes and heroines.

2. Make up some "Who Am I?" quiz questions about health heroes. For example, "I am given credit for discovering the germ theory. A method of purifying milk, which I discovered, is named after me. Who am I?"

3. Make a list of some things you are interested in, such as "How to be popular," "How to act at a party," "How to be a good sport," and "How to build a strong body." Find the sections in *You and Others* that help you with these problems.

4. Make a booklet giving information about how your community protects your health.

A Pronunciation Guide

The meanings of new words in this book are explained as they are used, but you may need help in pronouncing some of these words. For the pronunciation of the words listed below, follow the key at the bottom of the page (taken from *The Thorndike-Century Junior Dictionary*, obtainable from W. J. Gage and Company Limited).

abscess (ab′ses)
adrenal (ad rē′nəl)
autonomic (ô′tə nom′ik)

bacteria (bak tēr′i ə)
bacteriology (bak tēr′i ol′ə ji)

calcium (kal′si əm)
carbohydrates (kär′bō hī′drāts)
carbolic acid (kär bol′ik as′id)
chlorine (klō′rēn or klō′rin)
constipated (kon′sti pāt′id)
contracted (kən trak′tid)
cornea (kôr′ni ə)
cuspid (kus′pid)

dentine (den′tēn or den′tin)
digested (di jest′id or dī jest′id)
diphtheria (dif thēr′i ə)
disinfected (dis′in fekt′id)

elimination (i lim′i nā′shən)
enuresis (en′ū rē′sis)
epidemic (ep′i dem′ik)
esophagus (ē sof′ə gəs)
Eustachian tube (ū stā′ki ən tūb or ū stā′shən tūb)

filter (fil′tər)
fumigation (fū′mi gā′shən)

homogenized (hō′mo jən īzd)

incisor (in sī′zər)
incubation (in′kū bā′shən)
inoculation (in ok′ū lā′shən)
iodine (ī′ə dīn, ī′ə din, or ī′ə dēn)
iris (ī′ris)
isolation (ī′sə lā′shən or is′ə lā′shən)

Koch (kôн)

Leeuwenhoek (lā′vən hůk)
licence (lī′səns)

molar (mō′lər)

Pasteur (päs tœr′)
pasteurizing (pas′tər iz ing)
penicillin (pen i sil′in)
permanent (pèr′mə nənt)
perspiration (pèr′spi rā′shən)
phosphorus (fos′fə rəs or fos fō′rəs)
pores (pōrz)
protein (prō′tē in or prō′tēn)

reservoirs (rez′ər vwärz)
retina (ret′i nə)
rheumatism (rü′mə tizm)

sac (sak)
septic tank (sep′tik tangk)
sulfa (sul′fə)
sumac (shü′mak or sü′mak)
swab (swob)

urinate (ūr′i nāt)

Concepts

OF HEALTH, SAFETY, AND PERSONAL DEVELOPMENT

You and Others culminates the first six years of the basic program in health, safety, and personal development. It provides an excellent synthesis and enrichment of the important concepts touched upon in preceding books of the series.[1] Through text and pictures, the book presents fascinating information for eleven- and twelve-year-olds about the body and how it works, the effect of emotions on body functioning, growth patterns of preadolescents, factors underlying good posture, the essentials of good grooming, the need for and composition of an adequate daily diet, and proper methods of caring for the body and working toward sound physical and mental health. Safety concepts are considered in detail from the standpoint of safe living in the home, school, and community.

Built around the needs and characteristics, the experiences and feelings of typical preadolescents, *You and Others* really serves as a unique and much needed *junior guidance book*.[2] Common problems faced by children at this stage of development are touched upon—problems such as how to make and keep friends, how to be "a good sport," how to behave at social gatherings, how to cope with family frictions, how to learn to "take" failure, pain, and disappointment, how to understand better oneself and others.

Varying needs of the preadolescent readers are met by case-study incidents, cartoon situations, and anecdotes centring on the child characters in the book—characters who reflect the great differences existing among preadolescents in physical development, emotional and social maturity, family adjustments, and school achievement. All the stories and case-study materials serve first as a springboard to a discussion of the actions, motives, and emotions of the fictional characters—and from there to consideration of the children's own problems, feelings, and experiences. During such discussions the teacher may gain insight into emotional and personal problems requiring parent-teacher coöperation. In dealing with problems of this kind, suggestions in the Guidebook for *You and Others* will be most helpful.

A noteworthy aspect of *You and Others* is the emphasis on community health in the final unit, "You and Your Community." This unit develops increasing awareness of the work of the community in protecting the health of its citizens. The unit also develops insight into the mutual rôle of the individual and the community in fostering good health and sanitary living conditions. To clarify how a community meets the health needs of its inhabitants, the workings of a sample community are described in great detail. Included are the charting of the duties of the local health department; the story of how water is procured, purified, and pumped into homes; the methods by which sewage and garbage are disposed of; and the many precautions taken to safeguard the community's food and milk supply. Against this background, provision is made for the readers to think about, investigate, and describe the parallel health activities in their own community.

---

[1] Preceding books in the series are *Happy Days, Good Times, Three Friends, Five in the Family, The Girl Next Door*, and *You*.
[2] See the chapter on Preadolescents in the Guidebook for *You and Others*.

Unit One. You and Your Friends

That Square White Letter (pages 6–13)

Personal Development: In this first story are introduced the four main characters, whose experiences, thoughts, and feelings will be featured throughout the book. Like all preadolescents, these four children differ considerably in growth patterns, in interests, and in social and emotional maturity. These differences are suggested in this opening story, for each child reacts differently to the "square white letter"—an invitation to a party in celebration of their city's Centennial.

One Letter—Many Feelings! No Two People Are Exactly Alike, There Are Always Reasons, *and* **You—and Others** (pages 14–17)

Personal Development: We are all born with different capacities, and our experiences have made us different. That's why not all of us respond the same way to a given situation.

There are reasons behind the things we think or feel or say or do.

"You're Just Mean!" (pages 18–19)

Health: Rest periods should be interspersed with periods of strenuous activity.

Personal Development: In the midst of practice for the Virginia Reel Allen suddenly and without explanation drops out of the group. His action sets the stage for a consideration of what is "a good sport."

What's the Reason? *and* **A Good Sport** (pages 20–23)

Personal Development: All behavior is caused, and it is not enough to dismiss a person as being "mean" or "queer."

Indifference to the opposite sex is a common characteristic of preadolescents, especially boys.

Regardless of personal desires, there are times when it is only fair to be a good sport and to do one's share in a group project.

Hard at Work *and* **Feelings That Surprise You** (pages 24–29)

Personal Development: The Emotions. It's a good idea to stop and consider what makes us do the things we do—feel as we do—when everything seems to be going wrong. If we can find reasons for our behavior, we can check to see if it is appropriate and if it is practical. Better yet, after finding reasons for our behavior, we can often do something to change what we don't like. Just "letting off steam" by being cross, irritable, disobliging, sulky, etc., is not very helpful. Such behavior relieves tension for a little while. But it's better to find more worth-while ways of changing unpleasant feelings to pleasant ones.

"You Stole the Show!" (pages 30–31)

Personal Development: The day of the school program arrives at last—accompanied in the participants by such reactions as blushing, sweaty palms, or "butterflies" in the stomach! This incident provides a splendid setting for future discussion of how the emotions can affect body functioning.

Your Body and How It Works, Your Heart, Your Lungs, Your Skin, Your Adrenal Glands, Your Stomach and Kidneys, *and* Your Nervous System (pages 32–43)

Health: Elementary Physiology. These sections of the book provide a complete review and expansion of the following physiological concepts: how the heart and lungs work; the structure and functions of the skin; the structure and functions of the muscles; the function of the adrenal glands in giving the body greater power and strength when needed; the digestive process, including the elimination of wastes.

Also presented in these sections is material new to the series, a simple presentation of the *nervous system:* the *central nervous system* and its function of keeping us in touch with our environment and controlling our reactions to it and the *autonomic nervous system* and its function of regulating internal body activities.

Personal Development: The functioning of the body—breathing, heartbeat, digestion, elimination, strength of muscles—depends upon more than the way the body is built. The way we feel—excited, angry, worried, relaxed, or happy—influences body functioning.

(Note—New and difficult technical terms introduced in *You and Others*, such as *adrenal* glands on page 36, are explained as they are used in context—but their pronunciations are given in the Pronunciation Guide on page 274. The teacher should also note especially the supplementary lessons in the Guidebook, which give accurate and scientific information on the effect of *alcohol* and *tobacco* on such organs as the heart and the lungs.)

Wait and See, The Courteous Thing to Do or Say, *and* Think Less about Yourself and More about Others! (pages 46–52)

Personal Development: Social Behavior. We feel more comfortable when we know what to do or say in social situations. Consideration of courteous greetings, leavetakings, and ways of making and acknowledging introductions.

It often helps in social situations to think less about ourselves and more about other persons.

Instead of avoiding social situations in which we feel ill at ease, it's more helpful to try to find out *why* we are ill at ease, and then see if we can correct the causes underlying our behavior.)

Getting Ready, When Things Go Wrong, *and* How You Look (pages 53–63)

Health: Personal Appearance. Leads for discussion of what constitutes good grooming.

Personal Development: Grooming—a problem of little concern to many preadolescents—is often the cause of parent-child conflicts. These conflicts can be reduced if the boys and girls themselves will make a conscious effort to take a little more responsibility in these matters.

Frequently, however, preadolescent girls suddenly become exceedingly conscious of their appearance and anxious to "look their best." These children should be given aid in learning to do their hair more becomingly, etc.

Sometimes when things go wrong, body functioning is disturbed in some way; e.g., fear of some school subject may cause a stomach ache. It's always well to try to find out what's back of a headache, stomach ache, pouting, or "funny feeling inside." If the situation can't be changed, we must try to accept it.

The Party at Last *and* Going to Parties—and Enjoying Them! (pages 64–69)

Personal Development: Often by helping another person feel at ease and enjoy himself we can increase our own poise and our enjoyment of a situation. A deserved compliment also helps make another person feel at ease.

A good way to keep a conversation moving along is to ask a question now and then.

Leads for reviewing pleasant and courteous ways of greeting and taking leave of a host or hostess.

Unit Two. You and Your Family

"Being the Oldest Girl Is No Fun!" (pages 74–76)

Personal Development: Boys and girls who read this "case study" will be stimulated to talk over Elizabeth's experiences and feelings—and their own. They will be placed in a receptive mood for subsequent lessons which present desirable ways of coping with the feelings generated by real or fancied discrimination among members in a family.

Living in a Family (pages 77–79)

Personal Development: Feeling discriminated against is a common family problem. Among the ways of helping resolve the upset feelings thus created are (1) accepting the concept that "the fairest plan in a family is to have each help according to his age and ability," (2) seeing the advantages as well as the disadvantages of one's special place in the family, (3) "doing one's best" and not becoming unhappy by comparing oneself with others in the family.

Homemaking (page 80)

Personal Development: Another advantage in helping around home is the opportunity for learning the kinds of things everyone needs to know when he grows up and has a home of his own.

Setting a table correctly is a skill that will inevitably be needed.

When You Eat (pages 81–83)

Health: Food attractively served and eaten in pleasant surroundings has a beneficial effect on the appetite and on digestion. Cheerful feelings promote good digestion.

Personal Development: One way to deal with our unhappy feelings—feelings that may interfere with good digestion—is to get rid of the feelings by telling someone what is bothering us. Whenever possible, mealtimes should be kept free from quarrels, arguments, or airing of troubles.

Cooking Correctly (pages 84–85)

Health: Essential to "good" cooking is the understanding that *heat, air,* and *water,* improperly controlled, can take their toll of valuable vitamin and mineral content in foods.

The Safe Way to Do Dishes (pages 86–87)

Health: Every home should follow the practice of washing dishes *safely*—and that of handling *clean* dishes in a sanitary fashion.

Keeping Safe at Home (pages 88–89)

Safety: "Never touch electrical equipment with wet hands" is a vital safety precaution in the home. Leads for considering other safety precautions with electrical equipment.

"You Like *Him* Better!" (pages 91–93)

Personal Development: As they read about Allen, boys and girls will get the comforting assurance that they are not alone in having experienced such feelings as jealousy. They will be emotionally prepared to accept and expand the suggestions in subsequent lessons about ways of coping with these feelings.

Each of You Is Different (pages 94–96)

Personal Development: At times everyone in a family feels a bit "left out" of things or feels that others in the family are more favored. Such feelings are common and usually they soon go away. But if they don't go away—if they are buried deep inside —they may come out later in such disguised behavior as teasing, bullying, bragging, and "bossing." Showing such behavior toward a brother or sister should make you stop and think, "What is making me act this way?" Once you understand and admit your feelings, it is easier to do something constructive about them.

Do You Know How to Relax? (pages 97–98)

Health: By taking short periods now and then to relax, personal efficiency may be increased—for tired bodies do not function so well as rested ones. A little relaxing after a meal aids digestion—and short periods of rest between periods of strenuous activity give the heart needed rest.

Leads for discussing the sleep needs of eleven- and twelve-year-olds.

What's Your Hobby? (pages 99–101)

Health: A hobby can be "too much of a good thing" if it results in inadequate outdoor play and lack of contacts with friends.

Personal Development: Life is often much more interesting to those who have hobbies. But a hobby isn't a hobby unless we do it just for fun.

All about Yourself (pages 102–104)

Personal Development: These pages provide a usable setup whereby children can record pertinent data about their families, their friends, their favorite activities, and their feelings about important matters. The data thus recorded can be of great service in helping the teacher know more about the boys and girls in her classroom.

"Why Can't I?" (pages 107–109)

Personal Development: Boys and girls will be interested in the all-too-common problem of how to handle disappointments, and they will be curious to discover useful ways of coping with disappointments—ways that will be set forth in subsequent lessons.

When Disappointments Come (pages 110–112)

Personal Development: The best way of meeting a disappointment is to accept it and then see if we can't make some other plans or find some other way of having an enjoyable time.

When You Go Hiking (pages 113–115)

Health: On a hike appropriate clothing is also comfortable, protective clothing.

Safety: Consideration of safety precautions on a hike.

When First Aid Is Needed (pages 116–118)

Safety: First Aid. Every boy and girl should know how to give first aid in the event of minor injuries or ills, such as nosebleed, stomach ache, pimple on the face, cinder in the eye, insect bites, frostbite, and poison ivy, oak, and sumac.

The Foods You Need, Foods for Growth and Health, Foods That Protect You, *and* Foods for Warmth and Energy (pages 119–125)

Health: Nutrition. Development of how proteins, minerals, vitamins, fats, and carbohydrates help the body.

Planning to Get the Foods You Need (pages 126–129)

Health: Nutrition. There are certain basic daily foods that we all need to keep us strong, healthy, and relatively safe from disease. These basic food needs are satisfied if the daily diet is based on Canada's Food Rules as pictured on page 127 of this book.

"All My Plans Are Spoiled!" (pages 131–133)

Personal Development: Boys and girls who read about Jane's forced change in plans will be reminded of their own similar experiences and feelings—and will be eager to discuss what it takes to live happily in a family.

When Thoughtfulness Is Needed (pages 134–137)

Personal Development: To live happily in a family, we have to "give in" now and then to the needs and wishes of others. And we have to learn to "take" disappointments and occasional changes in plans without getting too upset or feeling too sorry for ourselves.

Safety at Home (pages 138–139)

Safety: The largest number of accidents happen in the home. Most of these accidents are caused by conditions that can be corrected.

When You Have to Stay in Bed (pages 140–141)

Health: Care of colds. The best treatment for a cold is plenty of sleep and rest in bed and lots of fruit drinks. It is also important to keep away from others as much as possible.

Personal Development: When we are sick and have to stay in bed, it is important to know interesting ways of making convalescence more pleasant.

Unit Three. You and School

Don't Try to Fool Yourself (pages 165–167)

Personal Development: We all have difficulties or weaknesses of one sort or another which we must learn to face. The first step in handling any difficulty we may have is to admit it—then see if there is anything to be done about it. Above all, it is important to learn to set goals that are reasonable and attainable for *us*.

Your Ears and Eyes (pages 168–169)

Health: Elementary Physiology. Our five senses are those of *hearing, seeing, smelling, tasting,* and *feeling*. Of especial importance to school work and to enjoyment of living are the senses of hearing and of seeing.

How You Hear (page 170)

Health: Elementary Physiology. Review of the various parts of the ear and their function in enabling us to hear.

How You See (page 171)

Health: Elementary Physiology. Review of the various parts of the eye and how they help us see.

Taking Care of Your Ears (pages 172–173)

Health: Review and expansion of how to give proper care to the ears.

Safety: Leads for reviewing ways of avoiding accidents to the ears through careless play.

Taking Care of Your Eyes (pages 174–176)

Health: Review and expansion of what is proper light for reading, with special consideration of the need for avoiding *glare* and *shadows*.

Development of awareness of the signs of eyestrain and of the need for consulting a doctor if these signs are often present. Review also of ways of preventing the spread of eye diseases.

Safety: Consideration of how accidents and injuries to the eyes may be avoided through using proper safety precautions.

Your Health and Safety at School (pages 177–179)

Health: Every school takes precautions to safeguard the health of its pupils. Leads for stimulating pupils to make a survey of the things *their* school does to promote good health and to suggest possible improvements in the setup.

Safety: Every school also makes provisions for protecting pupils from needless accidents or injuries. Leads for motivating boys and girls to make a survey of the safety precautions *their* school takes to protect its pupils and to suggest possible improvements that might be made.

"One of Those Things" (pages 182–183)

Personal Development: Doubtless Kenneth's predicament of dreading a visit to the dentist will awaken kindred feelings on the part of the readers. And a lively discussion may ensue about *their* experiences in anticipating unpleasant events. As a result of this "case-study" incident boys and girls will be awaiting with special interest the advice given in the subsequent lesson about making the best of difficult or unpleasant situations.

Making the Best of Things (pages 184–185)

Personal Development: When facing unpleasant situations it helps to realize that we all have to put up with some things that aren't exactly the way we would like them. It also helps if we try to find something good in a situation and think about that instead of continually fussing about the unpleasant side.

All about Your Teeth (page 186)

Health: Aching teeth make it hard for us to work or play as usual. Learning proper care of the teeth can help us avoid much unnecessary tooth trouble. Leads for reviewing the values of having strong, healthy teeth, e.g., they help us chew food properly, they make us more attractive, they enable us to pronounce letters such as f, g, j, and s distinctly.

How Your Teeth Grow (pages 187–189)

Health: Elementary Physiology. Development of the story of how the teeth grow from sacs present in the jawbone at birth, until a complete set of permanent teeth have formed many years later.

What Causes Teeth to Decay? (pages 190–191)

Health: Most dental-research workers believe that decay gets started as a result of sweet and starchy foods, which cause certain acids to be formed on the teeth. These acids make cavities in the teeth.

Consideration of how decay starts, how it spreads, why early dental care is necessary for a cavity, how abscesses form, and why the dentist uses the X ray when he examines the teeth.

Taking Care of Your Teeth (pages 192–193)

Health: Review and expansion of important concepts concerned with proper care of the teeth.

"I Failed the Test!" (pages 194–195)

Personal Development: It will be decidedly comforting to boys and girls to read of Jane's failure and to know that others, even children in books, fail at times, too. Some pupils may be motivated at this point to discuss times when they have experienced a total failure like Jane's. Curiosity will also be aroused for the next lesson, which expands the idea that a failure is not a disgrace if we have honestly tried hard and done our best. This next lesson also gives some other valuable suggestions about ways that help one get along more happily at school.

Getting Along at School (pages 196–199)

Health: Grooming. The knowledge that we look "right" for school and that we are clean, neat, and appropriately dressed can be very satisfying.

Personal Development: Consideration of some important aims to keep in mind in making school life pleasant and more satisfying.

"The Whole Story" (pages 204–207)

As their contribution to a school health exhibit, Allen and his classmates assemble a series of posters entitled "Keeping Healthy—What *You* Should Do." But under Jane's insistent prodding they gradually come to see that this set of posters tells but part of the story of good health in the community—and that the whole story involves not only the things each individual should do to keep healthy but the things the community, in turn, must do to safeguard the health and welfare of its people.

The Work of the Health Department (pages 208–211)

Health: Many communities are served by a local health department. The main duties of the local health department are to improve public sanitary and health conditions and to help check the spread of disease.

Your Local Health Department (pages 211–214)

Health: Health departments vary in size, but regardless of size, the main duties of any health department are much the same.

Preventing Communicable Diseases (pages 215–218)

Health: A health department has careful rules and regulations designed to help check the spread of communicable diseases.

What You and Your Family Can Do (pages 218–219)

Health: The responsibility of individuals and their families includes the securing of protective vaccinations and inoculations, reporting cases of communicable disease, and obeying all health-department instructions.

The Community Water Supply (page 220)

Health: Provision is made here for children to raise questions about their community water supply—questions that will subsequently be answered.

Where the Water Comes From (pages 220–221)

Health: Some cities procure their water from nearby lakes or rivers, others build huge storage places, or reservoirs, miles away and bring water into the city from these reservoirs. Still other cities get their water from artesian wells.

How the Water Is Made Pure (pages 221–223)

Health: The two chief ways that communities make the water supply pure are by filtering it, and by adding chemicals such as chlorine to it. Sometimes a combination of methods is used.

How Drinking Water Is Tested (page 224)

Health: To be sure that drinking water is safe, the local health department has samples of the water tested.

How Country Homes Get Water (page 225)

Health: Wells and cisterns usually provide water for people who have no city water system. Frequent testing of water from wells is important, and new wells should be lined with pipe casings and drilled deep enough to avoid contamination from underground drainage.

You and Your Drinking Water (page 226)

Health: Provision is made in this lesson for promoting investigation of the water supply in the children's own community.

How Sewage Is Carried Away (pages 227–229)

Health: Used water, together with wastes from human bodies, is called sewage and is carried away through the town's sewerage system.

Safety: Sewers must be ventilated because of explosive and poisonous gases that often form in sewer mains; and sinks and washbowls must be equipped with a trap to prevent sewer gas from "backing up" into pipes.

The Sewage-Treatment Plant (pages 230–232)

Health: Emptying sewage into lakes, rivers, and streams is a common way of getting rid of it. First, however, the sewage should be treated to destroy harmful bacteria in it. Sewage-treatment plants vary somewhat, but their main purpose is the same—that of killing harmful bacteria.

Sewage from Country Homes (pages 233–234)

Health: Homes not connected with a city water system use septic tanks, chemical closets, or outdoor toilets of various kinds. Proper sanitary precautions are essential with all such methods of taking care of wastes.

Sewage in Your Community (page 234)

Health: Provision is made in this lesson for stimulating curiosity about the details of the sewage system or other means of sewage disposal in the children's own community.

Garbage and Rubbish (pages 235–239)

Health: To be satisfactory, a city garbage-collection service should be regular and should cover the entire city.

Methods used to dispose of garbage are *piling it in the city dump, burning it, grinding it in kitchen grinders, and using the sanitary land fill.*

Garbage Disposal in Your Community (page 240)

Health: Provision is made here for evaluating the methods of garbage disposal in the children's own homes and in their community.

Fighting Flies and Rats (pages 241–243)

Health: Flies are dangerous because they can spread the germs of typhoid fever, intestinal diseases, and tuberculosis. Consideration of how to fight the menace of flies.

Rats are dangerous because they can spread the germs of typhus fever and a disease called the plague. Rats are also very destructive and cause millions of dollars' damage every year. Consideration of how to fight rats.

Safe Foods for the Community (pages 244–247)

Health: To be sure that foods are healthful and to prevent the spread of disease through foods, the local health department makes inspections of food stores, bakeries, food factories, and eating places.

Keeping Your Food Safe (page 248)

Health: Provision is made in this lesson for awakening children's interest in the ways their own community functions to help protect their food.

Safeguarding the Milk (pages 249–253)

Health: From the time milk comes from the cows until it is delivered to the dairies in town, every effort must be made to keep it clean and cool. At the dairy the milk is pasteurized—a process by which milk is usually heated to 142-145 degrees and kept there for at least half an hour. This process kills all harmful bacteria that might be present in the milk.

Your Milk Supply (pages 254–255)

Health: Most milk containers have labels which give considerable information about the milk.

To make sure milk sold in a community is safe, the local health department sends samples to the laboratory to be tested.

The home, too, should practise care in keeping the milk supply safe.

"Health Heroes," Anton van Leeuwenhoek, Edward Jenner, Louis Pasteur, Joseph Lister, Robert Koch, *and* Walter Reed (pages 258–264)

Health: Six men made some of the early and very important discoveries leading to increased progress in the war against disease. A microscope powerful enough to show bacteria, vaccination against smallpox, discovery of the germ theory, the beginning of antiseptic surgery, first experiments in bacteriology, and discovery of the cause of yellow fever are among the contributions of the six "health heroes" described in this section.

"Your Community—and You" (pages 265–271)

Health: Avoiding the spread of germs that cause disease is very important in making a community a more healthful place in which to live. But each individual should also make an effort to keep in the best possible physical condition. For a truly healthy community must be made up of healthy individuals, reasonably capable of resisting disease.

Safety: Individuals as well as the community itself must take responsibility for making the community safer.

Personal Development: Every individual should share in the responsibility of making the community a pleasanter place in which to live.

Index

288